UNION INTERNATIONALE DES SCIENCES PRÉHISTORIQUES ET PROTOHISTORIQUES
INTERNATIONAL UNION FOR PREHISTORIC AND PROTOHISTORIC SCIENCES

PROCEEDINGS OF THE XV WORLD CONGRESS (LISBON, 4-9 SEPTEMBER 2006)
ACTES DU XV CONGRÈS MONDIAL (LISBONNE, 4-9 SEPTEMBRE 2006)

Series Editor: Luiz Oosterbeek

VOL. 46

Session C75

Archaeologists without Boundaries: Towards a History of International Archaeological Congresses (1866-2006)

Archéologues sans frontières : Pour une histoire des Congrès archéologiques internationaux (1866-2006)

Edited by

Mircea Babes
Marc-Antoine Kaeser

BAR International Series 2046
2009

Published in 2016 by
BAR Publishing, Oxford

BAR International Series 2046

Proceedings of the XV World Congress of the International Union for Prehistoric and Protohistoric Sciences / Actes du XV Congrès Mondial de l'Union Internationale des Sciences Préhistoriques et Protohistoriques
Archaeologists without Boundaries: Towards a History of International Archaeological Congresses (1866-2006) / Archéologues sans frontières : Pour une histoire des Congrès archéologiques internationaux (1866-2006)

ISBN 978 1 4073 0622 3

© The editors and contributors severally and the Publisher 2009

Outgoing President: Vítor Oliveira Jorge; Outgoing Secretary General: Jean Bourgeois
Congress Secretary General: Luiz Oosterbeek (Series Editor)
Incoming President: Pedro Ignacio Shmitz; Incoming Secretary General: Luiz Oosterbeek
Volume Editors: Mircea Babes and Marc-Antoine Kaeser

Signed papers are the responsibility of their authors alone.
Les texts signés sont de la seule responsabilité de ses auteurs.
Contacts : Secretary of U.I.S.P.P. – International Union for Prehistoric and Protohistoric Sciences, Instituto Politécnico de Tomar, Av. Dr. Cândido Madureira 13, 2300 TOMAR
Email: uispp@ipt.pt   www.uispp.ipt.pt

The authors' moral rights under the 1988 UK Copyright,
Designs and Patents Act are hereby expressly asserted.
All rights reserved. No part of this work may be copied, reproduced, stored,
sold, distributed, scanned, saved in any form of digital format or transmitted
in any form digitally, without the written permission of the Publisher.

BAR Publishing is the trading name of British Archaeological Reports (Oxford) Ltd.
British Archaeological Reports was first incorporated in 1974 to publish the BAR
Series, International and British. In 1992 Hadrian Books Ltd became part of the BAR
group. This volume was originally published by Archaeopress in conjunction with
British Archaeological Reports (Oxford) Ltd / Hadrian Books Ltd, the Series principal
publisher, in 2009. This present volume is published by BAR Publishing, 2016.

Printed in England

PUBLISHING

BAR titles are available from:

        BAR Publishing
        122 Banbury Rd, Oxford, OX2 7BP, UK
EMAIL   info@barpublishing.com
PHONE +44 (0)1865 310431
FAX   +44 (0)1865 316916
        www.barpublishing.com

TABLE OF CONTENTS

Establishing Prehistory: The Foundation of the International Congress
    (1865/1866) 1
Marc-Antoine Kaeser

The 15th Congrès international d'Anthropologie et d'Archéologie préhistorique
    (Portugal, 1930) 5
Ana Cristina Martins

A Portrait of Flóris Rómer in the frame of Budapest-Lisbon CIAAPs
    1876 – 1880 Congresses 11
Erzsébet Marton

The International Congress of Prehistoric Anthropology and Archaeology
    and German Archaeology 17
Ulrike Sommer

Les congrès internationaux d'anthropologie et d'archéologie préhistoriques
    (1866-1912) et la question de l'éveil d'une conscience patrimoniale collective
    (fouilles, gisements, collections) 33
Arnaud Hurel, Amélie Vialet

A Scandinavian view of the beginning of congress times 41
Jarl Nordbladh

Le début de la culture de cucuteni dans l'archéologie européenne 47
Nicolae Ursulescu, Mădălin-Cornel Văleanu

LIST OF FIGURES

Fig. 1.1. Edouard Desor (1811-1882)..2
Fig. 1.2. Gabriel de Mortillet (1821-1898)...2

Fig. 2.1. Opening of the 9th CIAAP. Lisbon. 1880..7
Fig. 2.2a. Postcard. Excavated area of *Conímbriga*. 1930 8
Fig. 2.2b. Postcard. Excavated area of *Conímbriga*. 1930 8
Fig. 2.3. Postcard. *Citânia* de Briteiros. "Beautiful stone". 1930...9
Fig. 2.4. Draw. *Citânia* de Briteiros. "Beautiful stone". 1930.
 Museu Nacional de Arqueologia archives. Epistolário
 de José Leite de Vasconcellos. 616-4068A. 10/02/1931 9

Fig. 3.1. Rómer Flóris and Pulszky Ferencz. Portraits of the Prehistoric Congress/
 Arczképek az ősrégészeti kongresszusból/ Woodcarving published
 in Vasárnapi Újság/Sunday News, 8 October No. 41. 1876. XXIII.
 (Archives and Library of the National Office of Cultural Heritage,
 Budapest)...12

Fig. 3.2. Koperniczky, Broca, Pigorini, Virchow, Capellini, Hildegrand,
 Worsaae, Franks Portraits of the Prehistoric Congress. Woodcarving
 published in Vasárnapi Újság/Sunday News, 8 October Budapest,
 No. 41. 1876. XXIII. (Archives and Library of the National Office
 of Cultural Heritage, Budapest)..13

Fig. 3.3. Joseph, governor of Hungary, the patron of the 8th Congress.
 Woodcarving published in Vasárnapi Újság/Sunday News, 3 September
 No. 6. 1876. XXIII. (Archives and Library of the National Office
 of Cultural Heritage, Budapest)..14

Fig. 3.4. The respective national participation to the 8th CIAAPs
 Congress in Budapest, 1876 16

Fig. 4.1. Participants by Nationality...19
Fig. 4.2. Number of German delegates at CIAAP..20
Fig. 4.3. Oversees delegates to CIAAP 21
Fig. 4.4. Names of newly founded German societies, 1800-1920..24

LIST OF TABLES

Tab. 4.1. Congrès International d'Anthropologie Préhistoriques (CIAAP),
 dates and venues of conferences 18

Tab. 4.2. German delegates at CIAAP 27

ESTABLISHING PREHISTORY: THE FOUNDATION OF THE INTERNATIONAL CONGRESS (1865/1866)

Marc-Antoine KAESER

Director of the Latenium, Archaeology Park and Museum, Neuchâtel, Associate professor, Chair of prehistoric archaeology, University Neuchâtel, Laténium, Espace Paul-Vouga, CH-2068 Hauterive (Switzerland), marc-antoine.kaeser@unine.ch

Abstract: *The foundation of the International Congress of Prehistory (CIAAP: Congrès international d'anthropologie et d'archéologie préhistoriques) in 1865 played a decisive role in the establishment of the discipline on the making. Considering the context of epistemological conflicts in which this foundation took place, this article illustrates the motives of the instigators of the CIAAP. While the first national institutions and university chairs specifically dedicated to prehistory have been created around 1900 only, it appears that it is actually the CIAAP which allowed the establishment of prehistoric archaeology. Now, in this process, the choice of an international channel was far from accidental. Because, while setting the research agenda and the scale of analysis on a universal level, the International Congress entailed the heuristic setting of prehistory in the scope of an evolutionist epistemology, and the adoption of methods derived from the natural sciences – to the detriment of the culturalist and historicist perspectives of the antiquarian tradition.*
Keywords: history of archaeology – institutionalization – methodology – evolutionism – epistemology

Resume: *La fondation du Congrès international de préhistoire (CIAAP) en 1865 a exercé une influence décisive sur l'affirmation de notre discipline. Evoquant brièvement le contexte conflictuel dans lequel cette fondation a pris place, cet article illustre les motifs de ses promoteurs. Alors que les premières institutions nationales et les premières chaires universitaires exclusivement dédiées à la préhistoire n'ont été établies qu'aux alentours de 1900, il apparaît que c'est le CIAAP qui a autorisé l'institutionnalisation de l'archéologie préhistorique. Or la voie de l'internationalisation n'était pas fortuite. Car en plaçant l'échelle d'analyse sur un plan universel, le Congrès international a entraîné l'inscription épistémologique de la préhistoire dans le cadre de l'évolutionnisme, et l'adoption de méthodes naturalistes — au détriment des perspectives culturalistes et historicistes de la tradition antiquaire.*
Mots-cle: *histoire de l'archéologie – institutionnalisation – méthodologie – évolutionnisme – épistémologie*

History of archaeology has developed very fast during the last decade (Trigger, 2001; Murray, 2002; Schlanger, 2002; Trigger, 2006). As regards prehistory, historiography is characterized by a great diversity. Schematically, present researches into the history of prehistoric archaeology follow two radically different paths. The first one, which relies upon a critical stance towards the politics of research in the past (as well as in the present), can be labelled as a kind of social history of archaeology. The second one, which aims at an epistemological understanding of the development of the discipline, rather belongs to the history of ideas. Now, the divergence between these two approaches has made it quite difficult for historians of archaeology to cooperate on a common ground; all the more so, since most of the research is not carried out by professional historians, but usually by archaeologists who act as historians.

Under those circumstances, the study of institutions (such as the International Congress of Prehistory) can prove especially useful. As a matter of fact, science studies have demonstrated the decisive role played by the institutions in the establishment of the disciplines. Institutions actually account for the policy of science and for the agenda of research; they control the validity of the methods; they offer the heuristic incentive and the material framwork of the study, and impart visibility to the research field (Blanckaert, 1995). Thus, they provide for the production, diffusion, and reproduction of specialized knowledge. Their property to link the cognitive factors together with the sociohistorical elements in the construction of science makes their study especially interesting for historians, because they allow to go beyond the sterile oppositions between sociology of science and history of ideas.

With regard to the beginnings of prehistoric science, the role of institutions was to be all the more important, considering the wideness of the discipline's epistemological origins. As a matter of fact, it is common knowledge that prehistoric research is the result of a merging of a lot of distinct research fields[1] and traditions: previous to its institutionalization, it was carried out by scholars with extremely diversified intellectual and disciplinary backgrounds (history, philology, ethnography, anthropology, palaeontology, geology, botanics, etc.).

From this viewpoint, the International Congress of Prehistory (*Congrès international d'archéologie et d'anthropologie préhistoriques,* CIAAP), which was founded in La Spezia (Italy) and Neuchâtel (Switzerland) between 1865 and 1866, proves particularly instructive. Since it was the first institutional body in the field of prehistoric research, the CIAAP exerted a seminal influence on the discipline on the making. Enforcing the very name of "prehistoric archaeology", this institution played a decisive role in the shaping of the scope of

---
[1] On the difference between "subject of research", "research field", and (academic) "discipline", cf. Kaeser, 2006.

Fig. 1.1. Edouard Desor (1811-1882)

Fig. 1.2. Gabriel de Mortillet (1821-1898)

prehistoric research, as well as in the definition of the methods and the epistemology of the discipline.

Scrutinized from the behind the scenes, far from its official history,[2] the International Congress of Prehistory actually appears as the result of a complex intrigue, its founders (Edouard Desor and Gabriel de Mortillet[3]: fig. 1.1 and fig. 1.2) resorting to a whole set of manœuvres, in order to reach their goal, so as to shape the form, the aims and the orientation of the institution according to their own views (Kaeser, 2001; 2002).

On the ideological level, the CIAAP obviously conveyed the beliefs of its founders: in their eyes, true science was international by nature, and was to be shared within the "international republic of savants". Thus, after the Paris meeting in 1867, a free-thinker banquet offered to the foreign participants of the Congress gave way to eloquent statements: *"In the name of cosmopolitan science, international borders collapsed by themselves. Twenty times, enthusiastic bravos greeted the words of Fraternity and Freedom. Science has but one home: humanity!"* (Coudereau, 1867, p. 131).

Actually, the cosmopolitan and internationalist ideals characteristic of the second half of the 19th Century contributed to the foundation of countless other international congresses (Rasmussen, 1990). But in this process of internationalization, prehistoric archaeology nevertheless appears as quite precocious, largely anticipating the creation of similar institutions in far better established disciplines, such as geology[4] (1878), mathematics (1893), or physics (1900). This earliness is all the more surprising, when compared to the late institutionalization of prehistory on the respective national levels. As a matter of fact, the first national institutions exclusively dedicated to prehistoric archaeology were not founded before the beginning of the 20th Century — not to speak of the academic establishment of the discipline in the universities, which was generally reached decades later only (Callmer *et al.* 2006).

All the same, the foundation of the CIAAP did not proceed from cosmopolitan ideals only. For the ideological beliefs of its founders were closely connected to the epistemological commitment implicit to their idea of prehistoric archaeology. While setting the research agenda on an international level, they were paving the way for the affirmation of the evolutionist paradigm, which could make sense in a universal perspective only. Conversely, it allowed to thwart the assessment of the historicist and culturalist agenda of their antiquarian colleagues heir to the philological traditions of research.[5] For the creation of the International Congress of Prehistory took place in a clearly antagonistic context, which actually accounts for the tales of its official history. As matter of fact, the new institution lead to a clearing of the research field. In accordance with Desor and Mortillet's objectives, the participation of antiquarians in the CIAAP remained minimal, and was hardly noted (Kaeser, 2001, p. 219 sqq.; 2002). Prehistory could be

---

[2] For instance: Cotteau, 1889; Capellini, 1906, p. 14 sqq.; Nenquin, 1994. For reflections on the biases of such official histories (and their social role), cf. Richard, 1992; Coye, 1997, p. 116 sqq.; Kaeser, 2001.

[3] On Edouard Desor, cf. Kaeser, 2004; on Gabriel de Mortillet, cf. Richard, 1999.

[4] On the involvement of Giovanni Capellini, who had already played an instrumental role in the foundation of the CIAAP, cf. Vai, 2002.

[5] For a more detailed study of the two "research programmes" underlying the original idea of prehistory, cf. Kaeser, 2004, 291 sqq.

shaped by the representatives of natural sciences, according to their notion of a "natural history of mankind".[6]

In short, the CIAAP served to free prehistoric archaeology from the tutelage of written sources (sacred and profane), of oral traditions, and of the whole classical legacy. Defending a clearly naturalistic notion of the research field, the new institution stood up for the construction of a knowledge based exclusively on the archaeological study of material sources, resorting to stratigraphical, typological and technological methods, and closely linked with physical anthropology. At the same time, the adoption of this universalist framework helped to align prehistoric research with evolutionism. In contrast to the antiquarian programme which was primarily concerned with defining the diachronic permanence and the essentialist features of individual cultures, peoples, and "nations", the evolutionist programme sought to characterize the successive stages of the development of civilization. Now, since this explanatory framework sought to be universal and valid for the humanity as a whole, the organizational structure under which these studies compelled recognition could in turn only be international.

Bibliography

BLANCKAERT, C. (1995) – Fondements disciplinaires de l'anthropologie française au XIXe siècle. Perspectives historiographiques. *Politix*. Paris. 29, p. 31-54.

CALLMER, J. & al. eds. (2006) – *Die Anfänge der ur- und frühgeschichtlichen Archäologie als archäologisches Fach (1890-1930) im europäischen Vergleich. Internationale Tagung an der Humboldt-Universität zu Berlin vom 13.-16. März 2003*. Rahden: Verlag M. Leidorf (Berliner Archäologische Forschungen; 2).

CAPELLINI, G. (1906-1907) – [no title]. In *Congrès international d'archéologie et d'anthropologie préhistoriques, 13e session, Monaco, 1906*. Monaco: Imprimerie de Monaco.

COTTEAU, G. (1889) – *Le Préhistorique en Europe. Congrès. Musées. Excursions*. Paris: Baillière.

COUDEREAU, A. (1867) – Bulletin. *La Pensée nouvelle*. Paris. 1-17 (08.09.1867), p. 129-131.

COYE, N. (1997) – *La préhistoire en parole et en acte. Méthodes et enjeux de la pratique archéologique, 1830-1950*. Paris: L'Harmattan.

KAESER, M.-A. (2001) – L'internationalisation de la préhistoire, une manoeuvre tactique? Les conséquences épistémologiques de la fondation des Congrès internationaux d'anthropologie et d'archéologie préhistoriques. In Blanckaert, C. ed. – *Les politiques de l'anthropologie. Discours et pratiques en France (1860-1940)*. Paris: L'Harmattan, p. 201-230.

KAESER, M.-A. (2002) – On the international roots of prehistory. *Antiquity*. Cambridge. 76, p. 170-177.

KAESER, M.-A. (2004) – *L'univers du préhistorien. Science, foi et politique dans l'œuvre et la vie d'Edouard Desor (1811-1882)*. Paris: L'Harmattan.

KAESER, M.-A. (2006) – The First Establishment of Prehistoric Science. The Shortcomings of Autonomy. In Callmer, J. & al. eds. – *Die Anfänge der ur- und frühgeschichtlichen Archäologie als archäologisches Fach (1890-1930) im europäischen Vergleich. Internationale Tagung an der Humboldt-Universität zu Berlin vom 13.-16. März 2003*. Rahden: Verlag M. Leidorf, p. 149-160 (Berliner Archäologische Forschungen; 2).

MURRAY, T. (2002) – Epilogue: why the history of archaeology matters. *Antiquity*. Cambridge. 76, p. 234-238.

NENQUIN, J. (1994) – Une brève histoire de l'Union internationale des Sciences pré- et protohistoriques, et son organisation. *Bulletin du XIIIe Congrès de l'UISPP*. Forli. 2, p. 28-33.

RASMUSSEN, A. (1990) – Jalons pour une histoire des congrès internationaux au XIXe siècle: Régulation scientifique et propagande intellectuelle. *Relations internationales*. Paris. 62, p. 115-133.

RICHARD, N. (1992) – L'institutionnalisation de la préhistoire. *Communications*. Paris. 54, p. 189-207.

RICHARD, N. (1999) – Gabriel de Mortillet, 1821-1898. In Murray, T. ed. – *Encyclopedia of Archaeology. The Great Archaeologists*. Santa Barbara-Denver-Oxford: ABC-Clio, p. 93-107.

SCHLANGER, N. (2002) – Ancestral Archives: Explorations in the History of Archaeology. *Antiquity*. Cambridge. 76, p. 127-131.

TRIGGER, B. (2001) – Historiography. In Murray, T. – *Encyclopedia of Archaeology. History and Discoveries*. Santa Barbara-Denver-Oxford: ABC-Clio, p. 630-639.

TRIGGER, B. (2006) – *A history of archaeological thought*. Cambridge: Cambridge University Press [2nd edition].

VAI, G.B. (2002) – Giovanni Capellini and the origin of the International Geological Congress. *Episodes*. Ottawa (International Union of Geological Sciences). 25-4, p. 248-254.

---

[6] On the limits and drawbacks of the institutionalization through the CIAAP, cf. Kaeser, 2006.

THE 15TH *CONGRES INTERNATIONAL D'ANTHROPOLOGIE ET D'ARCHEOLOGIE PREHISTORIQUE* (PORTUGAL, 1930)[1]

Ana Cristina MARTINS

Tropical Research Institute, IICT – Instituto de Investigação Científica Tropical,
Rua da Junqueira, 86-1., 1300-344 Lisboa, Portugal, ana.martins@iict.pt

Abstract: The The 15th Congrès international d'Anthropologie et d'Archéologie préhistorique took place in 1930, in the Portuguese cities of Coimbra and Porto, in order, not only to commemorate the 9th session organised in Lisbon, in 1880, but to reorganize the anthropological and prehistoric studies, after a long period of inactivity due to the 1st World War. This paper constitutes a first attempt to understand the organisation of the sessions, as well as the themes preferentially explored in them.
Key words: CIAAP, Portugal, nationalism

Résumé: En 1930, la 15e session du Congrès international d'Anthropologie et d'Archéologie préhistorique eu lieux dans les villes portugaises de Coimbra et Porto, non seulement pour commémorer la 9e session organisée à Lisbonne en 1880, mais pour réorganiser les études anthropologiques et préhistoriques, après un long période d'inactivité décorent de la 1e Guerre Mondiale. Cet article constitue une première tentative de comprendre l'organisation interne des sessions, en même temps que les thèmes majoritairement explorer pendant les mêmes.
Paroles clés: CIAAP, Portugal, nationalisme

Resumo: Em 1930, tinha lugar, nas cidades de Coimbra e do Porto, a XV sessão do Congresso Internacional de Antropologia e Arqueologia Pré-histórica, não apenas para comemoração do cinquentenário da IX sessão realizada em Lisboa, em 1880, como para reorganizar os estudos antropológicos e pré-históricos, depois de um longo período de inactividade decorrente da 1.ª Grande Guerra. Este artigo constitui uma primeira abordagem ao modo como as sessões decorreram e às temáticas preferencialmente exploradas nas mesmas.
Palavras-chave: CIAAP, Portugal, nacionalismo

THE BEGINNING

During the commemorations of the fifty years of the realisation, in Lisbon, of the 9th Session of the "International Congress of Anthropology and Prehistoric Archaeology" (ICAPA) – 1880 -, it took place again, in Portugal, a new session with the same name, in September of 1930.

This occurred after a long period of inactivity following the First World War. In an attempt to surpass this situation it was created, in 1921, the "International Institute of Anthropology" (IIA). However, its goals didn't entirely meet the interests and needs of those working in the field of Prehistoric and Protohistoric research, besides the fact that it didn't include scientists belonging to the defeated block during that war. It was then that the Permanent Council of the ICAPA and the Executive Commission of the IIA combined efforts and decided to promote together the 15th session of the ICAPA and the 4th session of the IIA, in Portugal, restoring the original name of the Congress created in 1867. However, participation fell short from what had been expected, perhaps due to a predominance of anthropological subjects, in detriment to those exclusively archaeological. This provided the motive for a group of Pre-historians to meet a few months later, in Berlin, to discuss the organisation of an international congress wholly dedicated to the study of Prehistory, finally creating, in 1931, in the city of Bern, a new organisation entitled "International Congress of Prehistoric and Protohistoric Sciences".

PORTUGAL, NATIONALISM AND ARCHAEOLOGY

Independently from this, the session of 1930, activated even more, in Portugal, the direction of the studies towards the affirmation of the antiquity of human occupation in what now is Portuguese territory, especially since the chronology for Iberian Levantine Art was confirmed by excavations conducted by Luis Pericot (1899-1978) at "Cueva de Parpalló" (Gandía, Valencia, Spain).

It was the Asturian,[2] however, the favourite subject of the meetings, especially because the places identified, in the meantime, in Portuguese territory, were different from others even by the material parallels shown in relation to the French Aurignacian, Solutrean and Magdalenian.

This realisation was even more relevant because it presupposed quite a late development for the communities of the North-western Iberian Peninsula. Furthermore,

---

[1] We are grateful to Dr. Luís Raposo, Director of the Museu Nacional de Arqueologia (National Museum of Archaeology), in Lisbon, for all the facilities conceded to the writing of this paper, namely the consulting of the museum's archives and the publication of one of the illustrations (Fig. 2.4). ana.c.martins@netcabo.pt

[2] A macrolithic industry of the Mesolithic period of northern Spain, discovered in 1914 by the Conde de la Vega del Sella (1870-1941), known almost exclusively from *concheros* (shell mounds) at cave mouths in the coastal area.

foreign participants considered the Portuguese Aurignacian anterior to that identified, precisely in Asturias, since it included inferior Palaeolithic artefacts, placing it in the Acheulian. In terms of historico-cultural interpretation, this meant the late development in Portuguese territory, where it had been identified, in relation to the Cantabrian (Northern Spain), analysing the *picos*[3] (quartzite *picks*) as exogenous, belonging to a certain *Kultorvolker*.

Furthermore, this was a sensitive question amongst Portuguese academics, promoting collaboration between archaeologists and anthropologists on both sides of the Peninsular border, as announced on the occasion of the "Scientific Congress of Oporto", in 1921, whose advantage was:

> The **union and narrowing of relations between Portuguese and Spanish scientists**, often so far apart due to centuries of hate and rivalries of race and nationality. [...]. The two nations faced each other, as if in a great show: each presented their most distinguished scientists who, in their turn, demonstrated their scientific discoveries, in the exhibition of tools for the progress of sciences and industry (Tavares, 1921, p. 228).

This coming together began to crystallise, especially during the "13th Congress of the Portuguese and Spanish Association for the Progress of Science", in May 1929, in Barcelona. There, the opening speech of the sixth session (of Prehistory) was made, precisely, by the physician, anthropologist, pre-historian and university lecturer António Augusto Esteves Mendes Correia (1888-1960), on "*the problem of the chronology of the most ancient inscriptions from the Peninsular northwest*" (A.H./A.A.P., 1929). In fact, he strongly believed in the existence of *alphabetic forms* in Magdalenian artefacts and in Palaeolithic caves, since "*some of the engravings* of rock art of the northwest of the Peninsula *may be considered true alphabetic signs.*" (*Ibid.*), as he looked for irrefutable evidence of a Portuguese culture developed and profoundly rooted in Mankind's remote past.

And since the subject of Megalithism remained popular amongst the European scientific community, it would be the turn of an archaeologist, art historian and university lecturer, Vergílio Correia, to see a form of writing in the signs engraved on dolmens, such as those situated at Alvão, Trás-os-Montes (North-eastern Portugal), and Parada, Pontevedra (North-western Spain), as well as on portable artefacts, giving substance to a possible Prehistoric and Protohistoric communion between the regions of Galicia (North-western Spain), Minho (North-western Portugal) and Trás-os-Montes. Thus, it was identified the presence of numerical records of *things and facts – or accounting stones*, seen in stones with cup marks, and alphabetic signs on dolmens from Trás-os-Montes, where "Independently of form and usage, clearly symbolic, one may notice in those signs or their combinations an ***ideographic intent, the stenography of a certain language.***" (Severo, s/d, p. 738). Furthermore, to this researcher,

> *in a Prehistoric age, in agreement with a rough chronology, that is, well before the period attributed to the Phoenician invention, existed in this region of the Old World, linear signs representing a certain written language* (Id., *Idem*, p. 744).

But if the role assumed by Portuguese individuals at the Barcelona Congress did surprise, it was an unquestioned proof of their prestige in such a specific scientific field, at a time when Portugal witnessed the creation of the "Direcção-geral de Edifícios e Monumentos Nacionais" (General Board of National Buildings and Monuments – DGEMN). Simultaneously, there was a tendency for Archaeology to be managed by a single institution – the "Museu Etnológico Dr. Leite de Vasconcellos" (Ethnological Museum), which Director, the Professor of Archaeology, Director of the Faculty of Arts in the University of Lisbon, and for 30 years the official face of Portuguese archaeology – Manuel Heleno (1894-1970) – was sometimes disliked.

THE 15TH *CONGRÈS INTERNATIONAL D'ANTHROPOLOGIE ET D'ARCHÉOLOGIE PRÉHISTORIQUE*

It was during this period that the Administrative Council of the Associação dos Arqueólogos Portugueses (Portuguese Association of Archaeologists) accepted the proposal of its "Section of Prehistoric Archaeology" to take part in the 15th International Congress of Anthropology and Prehistoric Archaeology, whose sessions took place in Coimbra and Oporto, under the direction of the Honorary President of the Associação dos Arqueólogos, the founder, in 1893, and director of the National Museum of Archaeology and Professor of Archaeology in the University of Lisbon, José Leite de Vasconcellos (1858-1941).

However, the Congress didn't receive the same journalistic coverage as the Congress of 1880, not even attracting the pen of caricaturists not even the interest of politicians, or the publications of the proceedings. Fig. 2.1

It deserved, though, the interest and institutional support necessary for the excavation and conservation of the structures discovered in the Roman city of *Conímbriga* Fig. 2.2a-2.2b, under the supervision of V. Correia, with the objective of it being visited by the participants gathered at Coimbra, as it happened in 1880, in the shell middens of Muge (Mesolithic) and the fortified settlement (*citânia*) of Briteiros.

While member of the Congress (and, again, affiliate to the Associação dos Arqueólogos), the Priest and Prehistorian Eugène Jalhay (1891-1950), reproduced the work

---

[3] Poor in cultural materials, the Asturian industry it is characterised by a long, pointed unifacial quartzite pick (9th-8th millennia BP).

Fig. 2.1. Opening of the 9th CIAAP. Lisbon. 1880

presented at the Congress by J. Leite de Vasconcelos and by the soldier and Prehistorian Manuel Afonso do Paço (1895-1968), the latter on the Palaeolithic of the Minho, "[...] so *useful towards the ethnic determination of the human groups of the Peninsula during the Quaternary*" (A.H./A.A.P., Idem).

One of the greatest moments occurred during a visit to the "Citânia de Briteiros". This was caused by the discovery *in situ*, due to the effort of the soldier and archaeologist Mário Augusto de Vasconcellos Cardozo (1889-1982), of a "*beautiful stone*!", similar to that found in the 19th century, "[...] making patent an object searched for, that is its meaning." (A.H./A.A.P., 05/11/1930; Cordeiro, 1934, p. 160-172). Fig. 2.3-2.4.

It seems interesting that the only female paper, presented by the daughter of the Spanish archaeologist Juan Cabré Aguiló (1882-1947), M.ª de la Encarnación Cabré Herreros, was marked with the fact that it gave the Congress a happy note, at a time when, in the principal western countries, the role of women was winning greater importance in the midst of those societies.

This international meeting didn't achieve, however, a consensus between the (still small) Portuguese archaeological community. Truthfully, although it may seem strange, presaging practices still current amongst us, the Associação dos Arqueólogos wasn't contacted during the preliminary preparations. This is clear from the fact that the physician, archaeologist and university lecturer

Fig. 2.2a. Postcard. Excavated area of *Conímbriga*. 1930

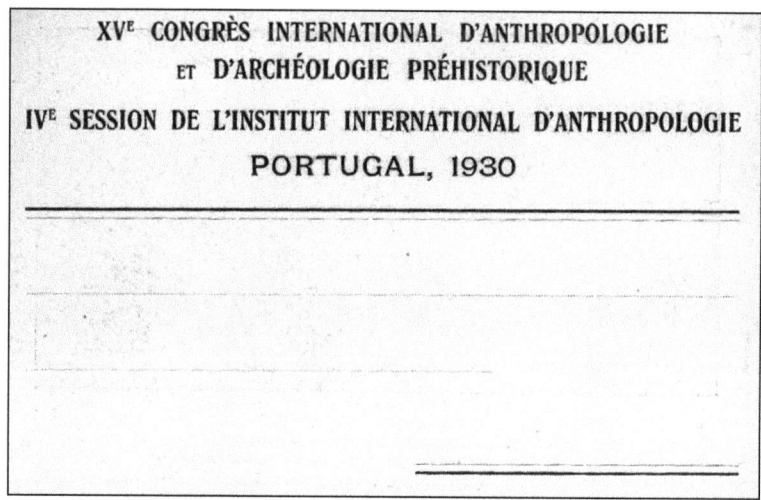

Fig. 2.2b. Postcard. Excavated area of *Conímbriga*. 1930

Joaquim Fontes (1892-1960), discovered its realisation in a National newspaper. Aside from this fact, J. Fontes disagreed entirely with the option, according to criteria still unknown to him, of organising the Congress only in the cities of Coimbra and Oporto, certainly through the influence of V. Correia and A.A. Mendes Correia, distinguished lecturers of those city's respective universities.

The reason for the disagreement was related to the fact that the programme chosen demanded that the sessions must concentrate in the north of the country. This was altogether surprising since Lisbon had archaeological collections, more interesting and important, *even unique in the world*, as the materials from the shell middens of Muge (Central Portugal), exhibited in the Museum of the Comissão Geológica (Geological Commission Museum), whiles the Museu de Etnologia, for instance, housed several Neolithic and metal artefacts. These observations were pertinent, at a time when,

The dense fog that enveloped Prehistoric Man, begins to clear; the figures on the other side are gradually more clear [...] [even though,] *according to an old custom, Portugal observes from the limits of the huge cave beyond whose opening Prehistory begins, and only much later follows the path taken* (Correia, 1912, p. 56).

It is certain that J. Fontes recognised – as he had to – the importance of the two cities as essential centres of Portuguese archaeological culture, mostly due to the efforts developed by their universities. However, he could not consider wrong the fact the Congress ignores Lisbon, precisely because it results in a total lack of knowledge of Prehistoric Portugal. As member of the meeting, E. Jalhay understood the reasons defended by A.A. Mendes Correia, that is, the need to harmonise the differences arising between the academic communities of Coimbra and Oporto, in their desire to both host the Congress. This issue, because it could threaten the realisation of the

Fig. 2.3. Postcard. *Citânia* de Briteiros. "Beautiful stone". 1930

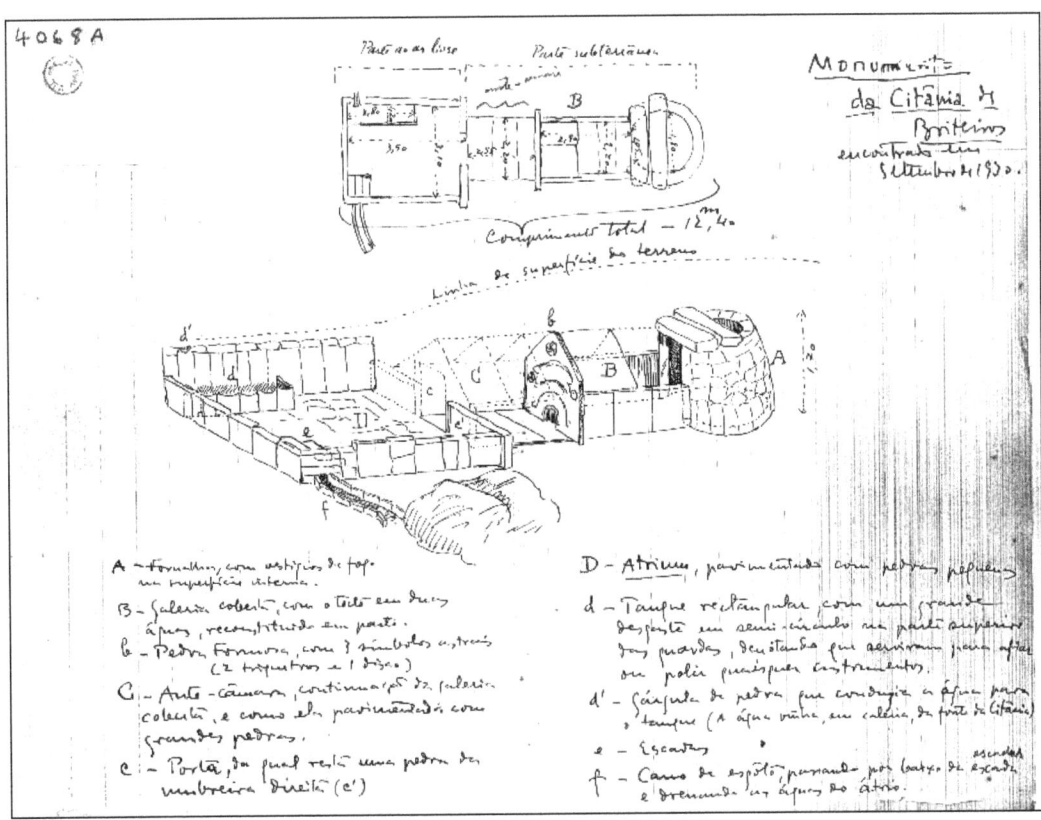

Fig. 2.4. Draw. *Citânia* de Briteiros. "Beautiful stone". 1930. Museu Nacional de Arqueologia archives. Epistolário de José Leite de Vasconcellos. 616-4068A. 10/02/1931

Congress in Portugal, was overcome the moment the Congress was transformed into a scientific event of unquestionable prestige for the host country.

The good sense of J. Leite de Vasconcellos advised "[...] that the Congress may be at Oporto, without the exclusion of Lisbon, that already had it in 1880. What matter is that

Lisbon will not be ignored? One must remember that, but without showing rivalries" (A.H./A.A.P., *Idem*, 22/03/1929). Besides that, it was to the recently created "Sociedade Portuguesa de Antropologia e Etnologia" (Portuguese Society for Anthropology and Ethnology), based at Oporto, that the Secretariat of the Congress addressed the organisational invitation, and it was at Coimbra that functioned the Portuguese Section (A.H./A.A.P., *Idem*, 22/03/1929.).

In any case, and as the example of the Associação dos Arqueólogos demonstrated during the previous century, the realisation of the Congress generated some National interest, inducing M. Afonso do Paço and A. A. Mendes Correia to participate in the 5th Session of the "International Institute of Anthropology", held in Paris in September 1931. Together with the Colonial Exhibition, the emblematic musealised spaces, such as the *Trocadero and Saint-Germain-en-Laye*, were visited. Furthermore, they presented papers at a time when the Colonial Exhibition,

> stressed our civilisation's role [...] and established closed contacts between the principles behind the colonial policy of Portugal and France, since the two countries *do not consider the indigenous population as servants, but rather as spontaneous and useful collaborators to the glory of the metropolis* (Paço, 1932, p. 40).

SOME LAST WORDS

In reality the Congress of 1930 induced members of the Associação dos Arqueólogos to present papers during the session of 1931 of the "Congress of the Luso-Spanish Association for the advancement of Science" (A.H./A.A.P., *Idem*, 26/05/1932).

However, although an apparent vigour characterised the organisation of the International Congress of 1930 by Public institutions (and consequently, with the support of the political power), the commitment of the Associação dos Arqueólogos itself and certain individuals, another *old custom* survived. In effect, contrary to what had been published in Portugal, the work presented by E. Jalhay on "Rock Art in the Northwest of the Peninsula" was published in the *Boletim de la Comission Provincial de Monumentos de Orense*, possibly due to its strong regional leanings, stated and legitimised, so adverse to the centralising intentions imposed by the political agenda of the *Estado Novo* ("New State"), regretfully it was,

> entirely forgotten that under the direction of lecturers from the Universities of Coimbra and Oporto, it has taken place in recent years at Condeixa and Muge (respectively), systematic excavations deserving the praise of foreign specialists that visited them during the International Congress of Prehistoric Anthropology, in 1930. Slides of the excavations were requested, as examples of the method used, by Count of Mesnil de Buisson, eminent Director of the French Archaeological Mission to Syria, to illustrate lectures of the course on field work given by him at the School of the Louvre, Paris (*Apud* Cardoso, 1999, p. 146).

Bibliography

Arquivo Histórico da Associação dos Arqueólogos Portugueses (A.H./A.A.P.).

CARDOSO, J.L. (1999) – O Professor Mendes Corrêa e a Arqueologia portuguesa. *Al-Madan*. Almada. S. 2, 8, p. 146.

CORDEIRO, L. (1934) – Cidades mortas. Uma visita á citânia. *Revista de Arqueologia*. Lisboa. 1, p. 160-172.

CORREIA, V. (1912) – O Paleolítico em Portugal. Estado actual do seu estudo. *O Archeologo Português*. Lisboa. 17: 1-9, p. 56.

PAÇO, A. (1932) – XV Congresso Internacional de Antropologia e Arqueologia Prehistórica. *Arqueologia e Historia*. Lisboa. 10, p. 40.

SEVERO, R. (s/d) – Commentario ao espolio dos dolmens do Concelho de Villa Pouca d'Aguiar. *Portugália*. s/l. I: 3, p. 738.

TAVARES, J.S. (1921) – O Congresso Scientífico do Pôrto (26-VI a 1-VII-1921). *Brotéria*. Braga. 19, p. 228.

A PORTRAIT OF FLÓRIS RÓMER IN THE FRAME OF BUDAPEST-LISBON CIAAPS 1876 – 1880 CONGRESSES

Erzsébet MARTON

National Office of Cultural Heritage, Budapest, Erzsebet.marton@koh.hu

Abstract: In 1876, Flóris Rómer (1815-1899) organized the 8th session of the International Congress of Prehistory in Budapest, which remains a milestone in the Hungarian archaeology. Rómer's main goal was the presentation of the unknown, unpublished but valuable prehistoric archaeological finds from the Carpathian Basin, a part of the Habsburg Monarchy this time. On display of the exhibition held in the Hungarian National Museum, he collected an extremely large collection, published in the periodical 'Compte-Rendu... Résultats Généraux du mouvement archéologique en Hongrie', which was founded on this occasion.
Keywords: 1876, 8th session Budapest – Paleolit investigations' start in Hungary – Copper Age – Ferenc Pulszky, Bronze Age Site – Tószeg, Virchow, Pigorini, Mortillet; 1880, Lisbon Conference – Rómer's participation, Schaffhausen's lecture, darwinism

Résumé: En 1876, Flóris Rómer (1815-1899) mit sur pied, à Budapest, la 8e session du Congrès international de préhistoire – un événement majeur dans l'histoire de l'archéologie hongroise. L'objectif principal de Rómer consistait à présenter les matériaux archéologiques encore inédits et méconnus mis au jour dans le Bassin des Carpathes, qui appartenait alors à la monarchie des Habsbourg. Les riches collections réunies par Rómer furent alors exposées au Musée national hongrois, et publiées dans la revue 'Compte-Rendu... Résultats Généraux du mouvement archéologique en Hongrie' fondée à cette occasion.
Mots-clés: 8e session du Congrès international de préhistoire à Budapest (1876) – début des investigations paléolithiques en Hongrie – âge du Cuivre – Ferenc Pulszky, site de l'âge du Bronze – Tószeg – Virchow – Pigorini – Mortillet – Schaffhausen – darwinisme

PROCEEDINGS

1867. Paris Congress – Flóris Rómer participated in the conference and the exhibition, where he presented the Hungarian obsidian, serpentine, flint and bronze archaeological findings.

1874. Stockholm Congress – decision on the location of the next meeting, which could take place in Budapest.

Between 1874-75, Rómer began collecting the archaeological objects and surveying the sites. Rómer's notes from 1874 – 1875 (XXXVIII.)

September, 1874. Rómer's travel from Breslau/Boroszló to Krakow/Krakkó (Rómer's notebook, XXXVIII. 39-40)

COLLECTED ARCHAEOLOGICAL OBJECTS:

Obsidian flints, bronze winged axes (Late Bronze Age) (XXXVIII. 47-48.)

Bronze axe, bronze decoration of a chariot (XXXVIII. 43-44.)

23 May 1875: Pozsony/Bratislava (XXXVIII. 83-84)

6 June 1875: Pátka-Malomhegy: tumulus graves (map) accompanied by Graffenried and Szenes Ede, beside the cemetery (XXXVIII. 89-90.)

Szécsény-Carpathian mountains – obsidian core, animal bones, pots (XXXVIII. 107-108)

Schlagendorf – drawings of fortifications (XXXVIII. 129-130)

13-15 August 1875: Rómer's travel from Poprad to Budapest

Sajógyöngyös: clay melting furnace (XXXVIII. 138-139)

25 August 1875: Móriczhida, Bakonybél, Somhegy, Dombháti erdő – Rampart, tumulus graves (XXXVIII. 150-151.)

27 August 1875: (Bakonyszűcs) tumulus, pots

28 August 1875: Bakonyszűcs, 100 tumuli – Rómer's drawing (XXXVIII. 154-156., 157.)

9 September 1875: Rómer's survey around the Balaton (Hungary)

Endréd: serpentine axe (XXXVIII. P. 185.)

Szántód: Serpentine object – fragmented (XXXVIII. 161-163.)

Zamárdi: fragment of a black-green serpentine axe, Kiss György's property (XXXVIII. 163-164).

Balatonszemes: dark green stone axe, fragmented (167.)

1875. Budapest – A National Conference of Prehistoric Archaeology and Anthropology was held in the Hungarian National Museum, organised by Flóris Rómer and Arnold Ipolyi. An announcement in the *Vasárnapi Újság* (Sunday News, a Budapest weekly) for collecting archaeological findings to be exhibited in the Hungarian National Museum, in 1876 September. An organising committee was set up with the participation of Rómer Flóris, Rónai Jácint (Benedictine monks) and Ipolyi Arnold (Catholic bishop).

Fig. 3.1. Rómer Flóris and Pulszky Ferencz. Portraits of the Prehistoric Congress/ Arczképek az ősrégészeti kongresszusból/ Woodcarving published in Vasárnapi Újság/Sunday News, 8 October No. 41. 1876. XXIII. (Archives and Library of the National Office of Cultural Heritage, Budapest)

3-11 September 1876, 8th Session of Congress for Anthropology and Archaeology, Budapest
Hungarian National Museum, Main Hall (that time the Hungarian House of Lords)

Opening of the 8th Session of Congress for Anthropology and Archaeology
Venue: the Hungarian National Museum – The opening speech of the Congress and the Exhibition was pronounced by Ágoston Trefort, minister for religion and education in Hungary.

On the corridors connecting the main hall, that time the House of Lords, the collected objects were on display. (Photos: Sándor Beszédes)

The exhibition was organised by a network of 120 members: county or municipal museums, museum associations and private collectors.

Rómer and his colleagues collected 31.500 objects, 22.000 items from the museums and private collections. 9.000 items were the property of the Hungarian National Museum. Most of the archaeological finds came from Cluj/Kolozsvár, mainly bronze objects. The University of Budapest was the second in offering objects, the third was the Archaeological Association of Oradea/ Nagyvárad, the fourth in the rank was the Protestant High School of Debrecen, and the Szabolcs, Vas, Békés county museums.

On display were also the private collections of Nyáry Jenő, Ebenhöch Ferenc-Mihályi János (stone objects from Transdanudia), Ráth György (bronze objects), Graffenried Arnold, Lehóczky Tivadar, Majláth Béla (archaeological findings of Bereg and Liptó counties).

Woodcarvings were published in the catalogue of exhibition (Compte-Rendus). 21 woodcarvings were

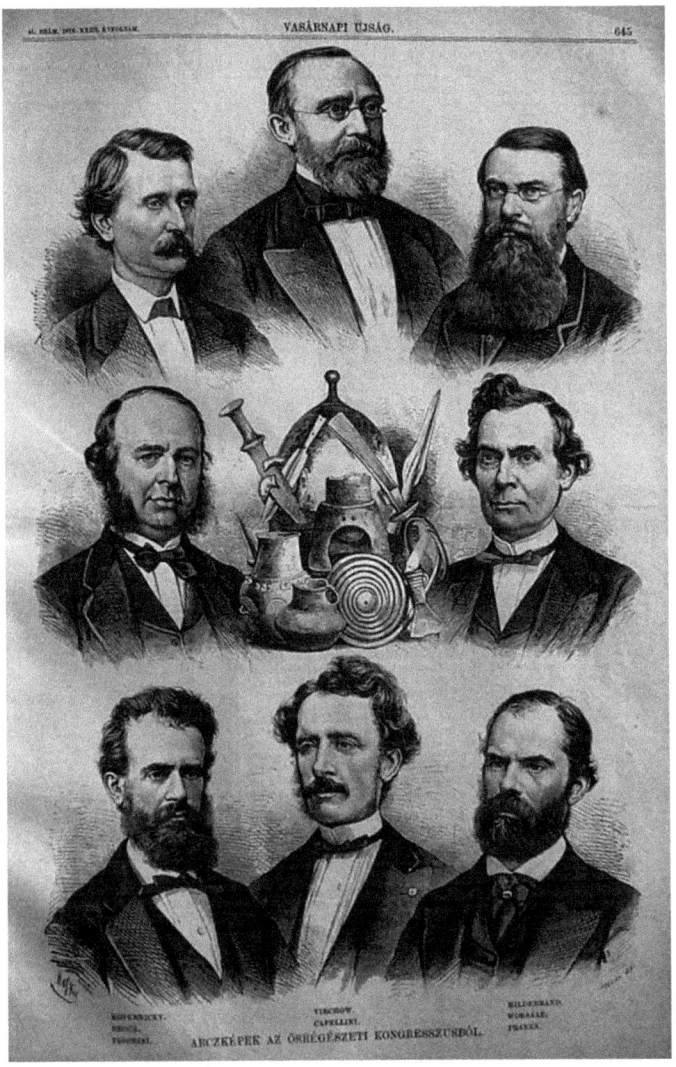

Fig. 3.2. Koperniczky, Broca, Pigorini, Virchow, Capellini, Hildegrand, Worsaae, Franks. Portraits of the Prehistoric Congress. Woodcarving published in Vasárnapi Újság/Sunday News, 8 October Budapest, No. 41. 1876. XXIII. (Archives and Library of the National Office of Cultural Heritage, Budapest)

published in the Vasárnapi Újság (Sunday News for the conference time).

VIP participants of the 1876 Budapest Congress
Sir Arthur Evans and his family, Worsaae, Montelius, Dr. Grewingh, Konrad Leemans (museum director, Leiden, The Netherlands), Lipp Vilmos (Szombathely, Hungary), Kovács János (professor in Debrecen, Hungary).

Scientific Committee: Rómer, Ipolyi, Rónai (Hungary). The working language was French.

Nine sessions were arranged. They were as follows:

1. The earliest evidence of human being
Bertrand (Saint-Germain, director, Museum of National Antiquities, France), comte Wurmbrand-Gundacker (Austria), Broca (secretary of the Paris Society of Anthropology) Jacquinot (Paris, France), Capellini (Bologna, Italy), Franks (British Museum, UK), Thomson (Boston, USA), Tardy and Zawisza (Warsaw, Poland).

2. The attributes of the stone objects in the Neolithic Age
Szabó József (Hungary), Belucci (Perugia, Italy), Broca, Baye (France), Montelius (Denmark).

3. The Bronze Age
Chantre (Lyon, France), Pulszky Ferenc (Hungary) – about a new period, the Copper Age.

4. The Iron Age
Henszlman Imre (Warsaw)

5. The Tumuli Graves

Fig. 3.3. Joseph, governor of Hungary, the patron of the 8th Congress. Woodcarving published in Vasárnapi Újság/Sunday News, 3 September No. 6. 1876. XXIII. (Archives and Library of the National Office of Cultural Heritage, Budapest)

Mierzinszky (Warsaw), Da Sylva (royal architect of Lisbon).

6. Fortresses
   Majláth Béla (Liptó county, Hungary).

7. Amber
   Dr. Wibergen (Sweden), Sadovsky (Krakow), August Franks (British Museum, UK).

8. Decorations – this session was deleted.

9. Anthropologic and Ethnographic Questions
   Hunfaly Pál (Budapest)
   Koperniczky (Warsaw)
   Dr. Lenhossek, Paul Proca (Paris), Dr. Schreiber Simon Arnold (that time a psychiatrist in Székesfehérvár, Hungary), Ujfalvy Jenő (professor in Paris, of Hungarian nationality).

SITES VISITED AND INVESTIGATED ON THE OCCASION OF CIAAP 1876

6 September 1876: Excursion to Gödöllő – Hatvan – Valkó

Valkó, 2 cremation graves were investigated/excavated from the Bronze Age.

Hatvan – Ökördomb, cremation graves came to light from the Bronze Age. 'The excavation of pots' was directed by F. Pulszky.

8 September 1876: Excursion by boat to Érd – Százhalombatta.

The participants visited the excavation of 2 tumulus graves under the auspices of Csetneki Jelenik Elek and Kereskényi Gyula and Luczenbacher János's excavation. The also surveyed BattaMatrica, the remains of a Roman bath (Civitas Matricorum), which had come to light a week before the congress.

10 September 1876: Excursion to Tószeg.
   Participants: Pulszky Polixena, Mestroff, Mortillet, Virchow, Pigorini, Csetneki Jelenik Elek, where they visited Csetneki's excavation (100x130 m² section).

11 September 1876: Excursion by boat to Magyarád – Bényi.

RESULTS OF THE 8TH BUDAPEST CONGRESS IN 1876

- *A new start of the paleo-anthropology and the Palaeolithic investigations in Middle-Eastern Europe.*
- *Copper Age being accepted as a significant period of Eastern Europe.*
- *A boom in the creation of museums, associations of museums friends and launching of periodicals in the country.*

11 September 1876.
Because 1878 was the year of the World Exhibition in Paris, Pulszky Ferenc entered a proposition for the next congress. Since for 1879 there was no candidate, the Congress in Lisbon opened in 1880.

RÓMER'S ACTIVITY FROM 1876 UNTIL 1880 (LISBON MEETING)

Source: Rómer Papers, archived in the Library of the National Office of Cultural Heritage, in Budapest.

Rómer's inheritance consists of I-XLVI handwritten notebooks about his travels between 1878-1888. In 1880, he became the canon of Oradea (that time Nagyvárad), thanks to his friend, Arnold Ipolyi, who supported the old, tired Rómer to get this position. During his years in Oradea, Rómer collected archaeological finds, until his death on 18 March 1889. His participation in the congress of Lisbon in 1880 seems to have been a beautiful break in his life.

SURVEYS AND COLLECTED ARCHAEOLOGICAL FINDINGS:

Rómer, notebook XL. 89-92.:
2nd June 1878
Picture 1: Zilah and its surroundings, the Szikszay collection. The objects came from Mojgrad, Krasna-valley, Dág, Szilas, a big mass of radiolarit flints, obsidian core from the "drum oriasci" (the giants' road, as the peasants called it – Rómer's notebook XL. 89-92.).

Picture 2: Magyar-Román Nyelvtan (Hungarian-Roman Dictionary), ed. Fekete János, with Rómer's notes. (Rómer XL. 32-33. 35.)

RÓMER'S NOTES ABOUT THE CONGRESS IN LISBON IN 1880

Rómer: XLII. notebook from March 1879 until October 1880.
From the 12 September until the 18 September 1880, he travelled to Lisbon by train via Udine, Southern France and Madrid. At the beginning of October, he travelled back home.
In some notes, he mentions the lectures of Riberio, Pigorini and Mortillet.
21 September 1880. He highlights Schaffhausen's lecture on Darwinism. This reading was the most visited session during the conference.
It is really interesting to read his description of Lisbon, about the glass palm houses on the avenues or the cows with calves in the streets of the old town. The opening ceremony on 20 September 1880 must have been very impressive, with the royal couple participating, not to speak of the beauty of Belem, Camoens, Thula, Alentejo and the sea.

RÓMER'S LAST YEARS FROM 1882 UNTIL 1888 – NOTES OF HIS ARCHAEOLOGICAL SURVEYS

28 April 1882. Survey in Dócz: 55 items, Roman silver coins, black handmade pots (Copper Age, Pécel-Baden culture), bronze fibulas (late Bronze Age – Early Iron Age) (Rómer: XLIV. 863/2)
1 May 1882. Végh Endre's mansion: bronze pin, arm ring, 4 'lunulas' (Rómer XLIV. 852/2)
30 June 1882. Rómer was invited to dinner in Debrecen, with nobles of the Monarchy. (Rómer, XLIV. 849/2)
29 July 1882. Esztár: radiolarit flints and tumulus graves. (Rómer, XLIV. 811/2
Esztár-tumulus: obsidian flints, loom weight. (Rómer, XLIV. 810/2)
29 July 1882. Henczida: mine, obsidian flints. Rómer XLIV. 809/2
Flóris Rómer died in March 1889, in Oradea.

Epilogue
After the excursion of the conference in 1876 and due to Gordon Childe's efforts in 1926-27, the University of Cambridge initiated the so-called Tószeg-project in Hungary in 1927

In 1876, L. Pigorini and Mortillet observed the similarity of the site with the lake-dwellings of Switzerland and the terramare sites in northern Italy. Pigorini's argument convinced other archaeologists, such as R. Virchow from Berlin, J. Mestorf from Kiel and I. Undset from Oslo, and Tószeg became internationally known as a terramare site.

In 1927, G. Childe started an excavation with Ferenc Tompa. New excavations (directed by Amália Mozsolics) were launched in 1949-1952, on the occasion of another international archaeological congress. The latest efforts were directed by I. Bóna and Ilona Stanczik in 1974.

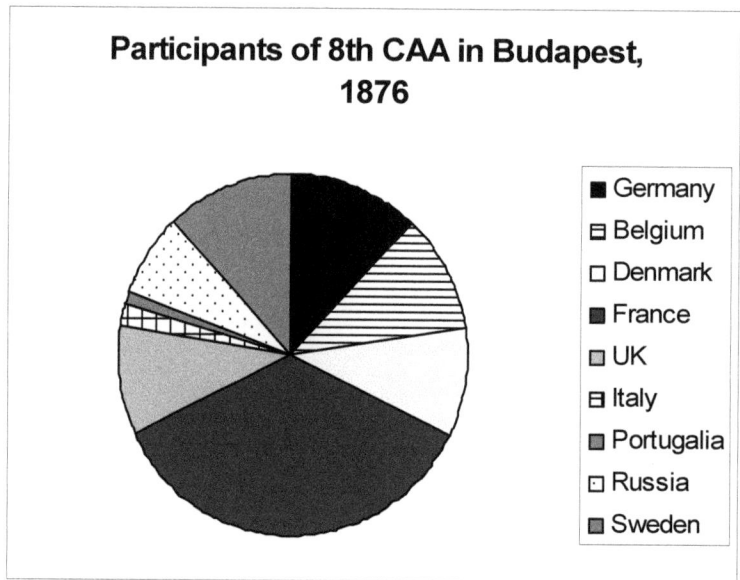

Fig. 3.4. The respective national participation to the 8th CIAAPs Congress in Budapest, 1876

In 2001, after the big flood of the Tisza, Tószeg became protected as a historical monument from the Bronze Age.

References

Vasárnapi Újság/Sunday News Budapest, 1876 September (National Office of Cultural Heritage, Budapest, Archive and Library).

Rómer Papers, handwritten notebooks I-XLVI. (National Office of Cultural Heritage, Budapest, Archive and Library).

Mary LEIGHTON and Marie Louise STIG SØRENSEN (Dept. of Archaeology, University of Cambridge): Tószeg (dissertation, manuscript) 2001.

Bibliography

BANNER, J., I. BÓNA, and L. MÁRTON (1959) – Die Ausgrabungen von L. Márton in Tószeg. Acta Archaeologica Academiae Scientificarium Hungarica 10, 1-140.

BÓNA, I. (1979-80) – Tószeg-Laposhalom (1876-1976). A Szolnok Megyei Múzeumok Évkönyve, 83-107.

BÓNA, I. (1994) – Tószeg-Laposhalom. In Bóna, I. and P. Raczky (eds.) Le bel Age du Bronze en Hongrie. Budapest: Zeneműnyoma 101-114.

BÓNA, I., and I. STANCZIK (1979-80) – Separatum from the Annual of the Szolnok County Museum 63-81, 83-107.

FOLTINY, S. (1969) – The Hungarian archaeological collection of the American museum of Natural History in New York, Bloomington. Indiana University Publications vol. 77, 25-32. The Hague: Bloomington.

FOLTINY, S. (1976) – Tószeg Pottery at the Peabody Museum of Harvard University. Bonner Jahrbücher 176, 27-32.

SCHALK, E. (1979) – Fundmaterial aus Tószeg im Naturhistorischen Museum in Wien. Mitteilungen der Anthropologischen Gesellschaft in Wien. 109. 131-146.

SCHALK, E. (1981) – Die Frühbronzezeitliche Tellsiedlung bei Tószeg, Ostungarn, mit Fundmaterial aus der Sammlung Groningen (Niederlande) und Cambridge (Grossbritannien). Dacia 25: 63-129.

//
THE INTERNATIONAL CONGRESS OF PREHISTORIC ANTHROPOLOGY AND ARCHAEOLOGY AND GERMAN ARCHAEOLOGY

Ulrike SOMMER

Institute of Archaeology, University College London, 31-34 Gordon Square,
WC1H 0PY London, tel. 0044/20 7679 1493,
u.sommer@ucl.ac.uk

Abstract: Traditionally, the influence of international Congresses (CIAAP) on the development of German archaeology has been seen as negligible. The conference never met in Germany, but quite a number of influential German archaeologists took an active part at CIAAP, and the foundation of the German Society for Anthropology, Ethnology and Prehistory can be directly linked to the influence of CIAAP. The international congresses were also influential on a more regional level, as can be shown by the example of the Hans Bruno Geinitz and the foundation of the Museum of Prehistory in Dresden (Saxony).
Keywords: History of archaeology – Congrès International d'Anthropologie et d'archéologie préhistoriques – International conferences – Antiquarian Societies – Worldfairs – Worldfair Paris 1867 – chronology – Deutsche Gesellschaft für Anthropologie, Ethnologie und Vorgeschichte – Hans Bruno Geinitz

Résumé: On considère généralement que les Congrès internationaux de préhistoire (CIAAP) n'ont exercé qu'une influence négligeable sur le développement de l'archéologie allemande. Pourtant, si CIAAP n'a jamais tenu de session en Allemagne, de nombreux savants allemands ont néanmoins joué un rôle important dans cette institution. La fondation de la Société allemande d'anthropologie, d'ethnologie et de préhistoire peut d'ailleurs être mise en relation avec le modèle du Congrès international de préhistoire, qui a également connu un impact notable sur un plan plus régional, comme on le verra avec l'exemple de Hans Bruno Geinitz et la fondation du Musée de préhistoire de Dresde (Saxe).
Mots-clés: Histoire de l'archéologie – Congrès international d'anthropologie et d'archéologie préhistoriques – conférences internationales – sociétés antiquaires – expositions universelles – Exposition universelle de Paris en 1867 – Société allemande d'anthropologie, d'ethnologie et de préhistoire – Hans Brunon Geinitz

INTRODUCTION

In the first number of the UISPP periodical "Prehistoria 2000" that appeared at the conference at Liège, there is a short account of the history of the "Congrès International d'anthropologie et archéologie préhistoriques" (CIAAP for short). We learn that the International Congress of prehistoric archaeology and anthropology "got cancelled because it privileged an anthropology that was not related to prehistory. The congress showed, on top of that, little internationalism in its organisation." (Prehistoria 2000, 14). In his history of German archaeology, Georg Kossack (1999) has not much to say about CIAAP either. "It originated from a specialised direction of historically oriented natural scientists." He adds: "It never convened in Germany or Austria." (ibd.), implying that it cannot have been very influential on German research if this was the case.

In his biography of Girolamo Cardano, a Renaissance savant and astronomer, Anthony Grafton (1999, 1) describes the writer of an autobiography as the "master of time", who "impresses shape and direction on events that, as experienced, usually lacked both." This, of course, is true not only of people, but of associations as well. In fact, the more I looked into the relation between CIAAP and the development of German archaeology, the more I was amazed at how much CIAAP had been written out of it – and at how well that has worked.

THE CONGRÈS INTERNATIONAL D'ANTHROPOLOGIE ET D'ARCHÉOLOGIE PRÉHISTORIQUES

The "Congrès International d'Anthropologie et d'Archéologie Préhistoriques" was founded in 1865 in La Spezia, Italy and met 18 times between 1866 and 1938. Originally, an annual meeting was envisaged; since 1872 it met only bi-annually, and after 1876 the rhythm became increasingly irregular, with an eight-year gap between the Meeting in Moscow 1892 and in Paris 1900 (cf. Tab. 1).[1]

The CIAAP was organised in sessions presided over by different scholars. There were no parallel sessions, and each Congress discussed a number of questions that centered mainly on chronology and methodology. In Bologna (1871), for example, the following questions were discussed:

1. L'âge de la Pierre en Italie

2. Les cavernes des bords de la Méditerrannée, en particulier de la Toscane, compareés aux grottes du Midi de la France

---

[1] I am not going to look at the post WWI-period, as the merger with the Institut International d'Anthropologie in 1927 changed the aims and organisatorial structure of the Congress, and the political environment had changed fundamentally as well.

Tab. 4.1. Congrès International d'Anthropologie Préhistoriques (CIAAP), dates and venues of conferences

	1865	**La Spezia**	Foundation as International Paleo-Ethnological Congress
1	1866	**Neuchâtel**	Official inauguration
2	1867	**Paris**	Coinciding with the World Fair
3	1868	**Norwich/London**	International Congress of Prehistoric Archaeology, English official language
4	1869	**Copenhagen**	French official language
5	1871	**Bologna**	Planned for 1870, suspended one year because of Prussian-French war. French only official language
6	1872	**Bruxelles**	Two-year rhythm introduced
7	1874	**Stockholm**	
8	1876	**Budapest**	
9	1880	**Lissabon**	Conseil permanent established
	1885	Athens	Congress suspended
10	1889	**Paris**	Coinciding with the World Fair
11	1892	**Moscow**	
12	1900	**Paris**	Coinciding with the World Fair
13	1906	**Monaco**	English, German and Italian permitted for lectures
14	1912	**Geneva**	
	1915	Madrid	Suspended because of WWI
	1926	Madrid	Suspended
	1927	Amsterdam	Union with IIA
15	1930	**Coimbra/Porto**	Spanish permitted for lectures
16	1935	**Bruxelles**	Coinciding with the World Fair
17	1937	**Bucarest**	
	1939	Istanbul	Suspended because of WWII

3. Les habitations lacustres et les tourbières du Nord de l'Italie
4. Analogies entre les Terramares et les Kjøkkenmøddings
5. Chronologie de la première substitution du bronze par le fer
6. Questions craniologiques relatives aux différentes races qui ont peuplé les diverses parties de l'Italie.

Normally, there were short presentations and extended discussion of the questions. Sometimes original finds were presented and discussed (or even excavated, like a "splendid cist" in the church of Marzabotto in 1871, Korrbl. DAG 1874, 152). Special Commissions were created to resolve specific questions, for example the existence of Tertiary man in the Miocene deposits of Charneca di Otta in Portugal in 1880. But the main purpose of the meeting was always, as Ignace Kraszewski (1874, 83) put it "…less the official séances but the exchange of ideas. Problems of language and distance are overcome by international meetings, and the delegate becomes acquainted with hitherto unknown research and countries." There always was a varied social programme, with dinners, wine-receptions, excursions, illuminations and fireworks. Normally the Heads of state did either welcome the delegates in person or sent high ranking delegates. The King of Sweden even took part in the conference itself (Kraszewski 1874, 31). Obviously, these international meetings were seen as an important venue to present the national achievements in the field of prehistoric research. Many accounts (e.g. de Mortillet 1867, 469; Mehwald 1869, 238; Carthaillac 1880, 15; Virchow 1880, 340) also emphasise the enthusiastic reception given to the delegates by the local population and "even" the peasantry, though this might not always have been wholly spontaneous.

French had been adopted as the official language both of the presentations and for the discussion 1869 in Copenhagen. This was presented as a matter of expediency. "Les langues du Nord ne sont malheureusement connues et parlées que par un petit nombre de personnes en dehors des pays scandinaves, aussi les archéologues et les naturalistes danois crurent-ils bon de faire savoir à l'avance que la langue française seratit plus répandue et plus généralement comprise et parlée par tous. Le succès fut complet et le nombre des membres étrangers présents

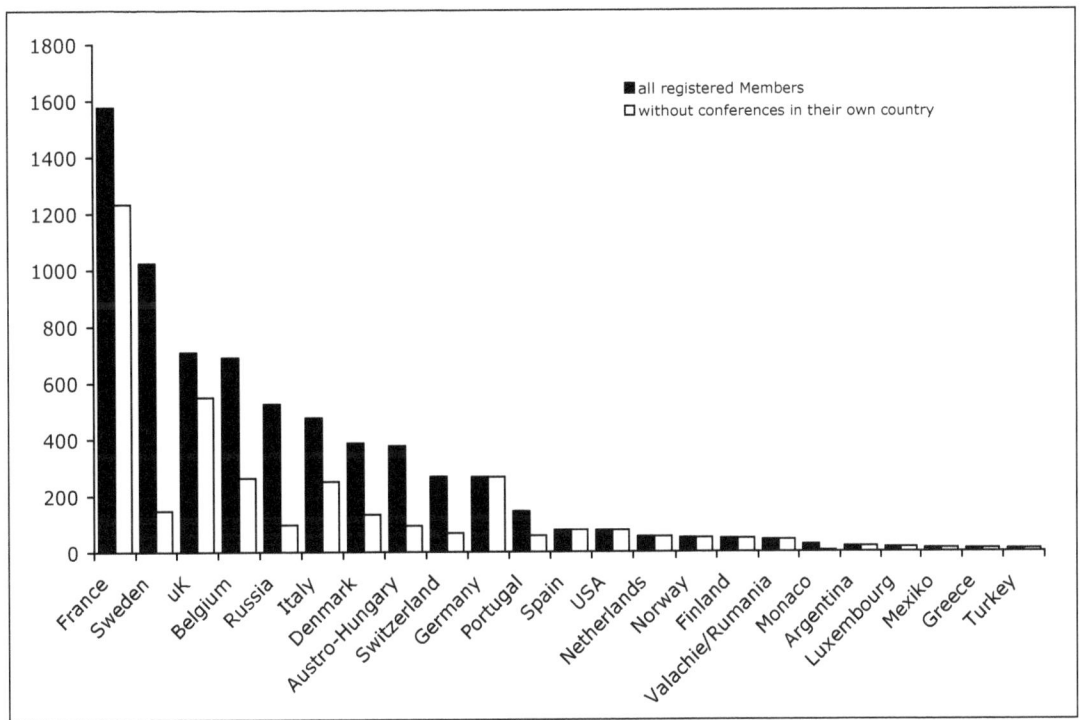

Fig. 4.1. Participants by Nationality

au Congrès de Copenhague dépassa de beaucoup celui des années précédentes." (Mortillet 1871, IX). But as S. Wiell (1999) has pointed out, there were political considerations behind the Danish decision as well. In 1864, Denmark had lost the Duchies of Schleswig and Holstein to Prussia and Austria, and anti-German sentiment was understandably still rife. In Bologna (1871), French was made the only official language of the Congress. "La langue française est seule admise pour les communications verbales pendant les séances et dans la publication et Compte-rendu du Congrès et des Mémoires qui y sont joints." Following in the wake of the Franco-Prussian war, and in view of the the hostility shown to German delegates at this meeting (Virchow 1871, 139) it seems likely that this adoption of French was a political statement as well. Despite numerous attempts to rescind this decision, only in 1906 were English, German and Italian permitted for the use in lectures, with Spanish to follow some years later.

France was the only country where the Congress was held thrice, Paris and Brussels are the only cities were it met more than once (two meetings each took place in Italy and Portugal, but in different cities). This influenced the organisatorial structure of the Conference, as previous presidents automatically became members of the Comité exécutif. France also was consistently the country who sent the most delegates (fig. 4.1). These statistics, taken from list of member and delegates in the Comptes Rendus, have to be taken with a pinch of salt, though.[2]

Sometimes only the number of subscription per country is given, and it is not indicated how many members actually took part. Müller-Scheessel (in press) assesses the proportion as 2/3-3/4.

Some people only subscribed to finance the congress. In Stockholm, for example, over 600 Swedes had subscribed to finance the Congress, "une œuvre de patriotisme et d'hospitalité" as Ignace Kraszewski (1874, 4) describes it. In London and Norwich, on the other hand, members of the British academy got in on a common ticket, so the numbers of locals may be severely deflated. In the case of women, it is often not clear whether they came for the conference, or as companions to their husbands or fathers, without taking actually part in the meetings. Johanna Mestorf, director of the Kiel museum, who visited nearly all conferences and wrote detailed reports, certainly was a participant. Hermann Schaaffhausen, Professor of anatomy in Bonn, in later years often travelled with his whole family, but this of course does not necessarily imply that "the Ladies Schaaffhausen" were not interested in prehistory. But as a separate Commité des Dames was established in Geneva, this certainly was not always the case.

The number of national delegates was mentioned in most accounts of the conferences, and was clearly important to many scholars. For example, in 1880, in his account of the CIAAP in Lisbon, Rudolf Virchow states: "For the first time since these Congresses exist, we Germans have been somewhat better represented, we even were, except for the French, the second most numerous nation." But he has to add: "As we were only 9 male representatives, but numerous females were present, you can see that the

---
[2] Some Members are attributed to the wrong country, this has been corrected when possible.

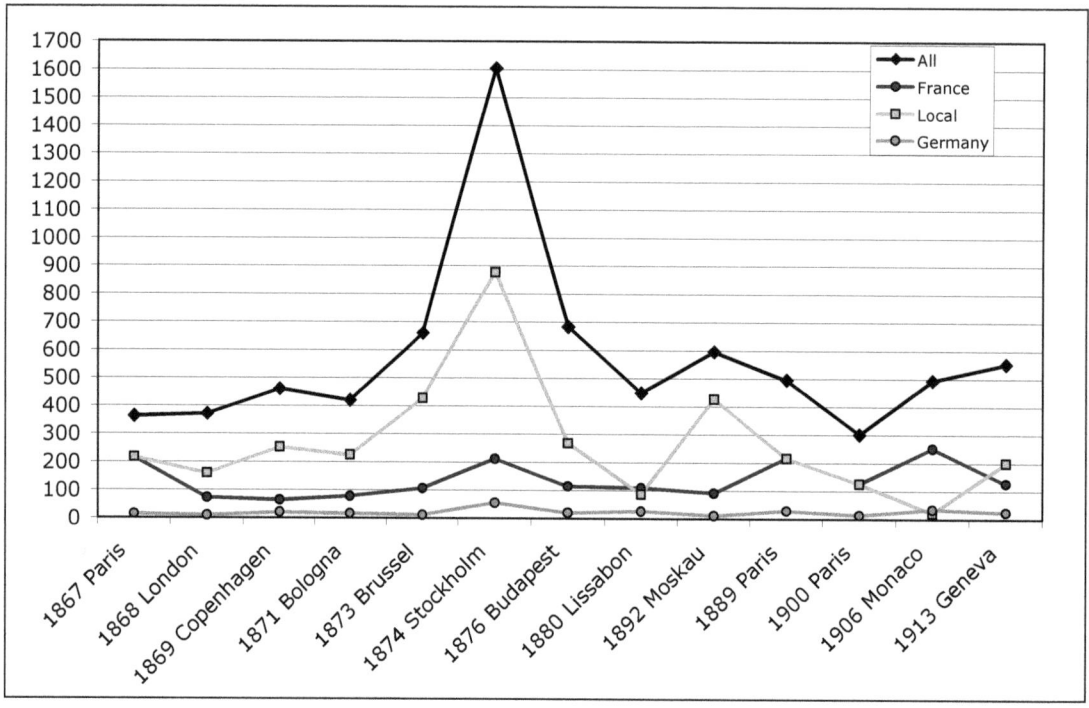

Fig. 4.2. Number of German delegates at CIAAP

Congress was not well visited, as was only to be expected with the great distance. But at least all bigger nations were represented."[3]

While the number of German delegates was not very high, it is not extremely low either (fig. 4.2). As can be seen in Table 2, the delegates consisted of professionals to a high degree, and most of them attended the meetings regularly.

The French "dominance" can be at least partly explained by the high number of professional anthropologists and archaeologists in this country that was leading in prehistoric, especially Palaeolithic research at that time. The language might have played a role, but at this time, French still was the major international language.

Between 16 and 25 countries were represented at CIAAP. The meetings always were a predominantly European affair (fig. 4.3), only in Paris 1900 and Geneva 1912 were non-Europeans present in any quantity, but still formed a small minority.

In Germany, the conferences were announced in all mayor prehistoric publications, especially in the proceedings of the DAG, and its president Rudolf Virchow always encouraged, sometimes actively enjoined people to attend.[4] In 1899, Johann Ranke again pointed out the "fundamental importance" of CIAAP for the "development of our subject" and warmly enjoined the members to participate in the forthcoming Paris conference (Korrbl. DAG 30, 1899, 66). While the Congress never met in Germany, German delegates chaired sessions and special committees. In 1900, Virchow was made a honorary member of the CIAAP (vice-président honoraire), thus presumably getting a seat on the executive council as well.

GERMAN ANTIQUARIAN SOCIETIES

Owing to the peculiarities of German history, basically a "failed Nation" between 1815 and 1871, there was no pan-German archaeological society until 1869. There had been numerous attempts at establishing such an association. After 1815, this was strongly discouraged by both the Prussian and Austrian governments. In 1829, Franz von Metternich, the de-facto ruler of central Europe, claimed that "any convention of scholars and writers from the historical and political disciplines will unfailingly lead to ominous and dangerous activities, even if not originally intended as such."[5] (Jacobeit 1965, 33).

---

[3] "Wir Deutschen waren zum ersten Mal, seitdem diese Congresse bestehen, etwas stärker vertreten; wir bildeten sogar nach den Franzosen unter den auswärtigen Mitgliedern die zweitstärkste Nation. Da wir jedoch nur 9 männliche Mitglieder waren – weiblicherseits waren wir freilich auch sehr gut vertreten – so sehen sie daraus, dass der Congress, wie bei der grossen Entfernung auch nicht anders zu erwarten, im Ganzen schwach besucht war; immerhin waren ziemlich alle grösseren Länder vertreten."

[4] "2. Der Vorsitzende [Virchow] legt das Programm des diesjährigen, in Stockholm vom 7.-17. August stattfindenden internationalen Congresses für prähistorische Archäologie und Anthropologie vor und ermahnt zur regen Teilnahme." (Verhandlungen BAG 1874, 26, Minutes of the first meeting).

[5] "...daß eine Zusammenkunft von Gelehrten und Schriftstellern in den historischen und politischen Fächern unfehlbar zu bedenklichen und gefährlichen Umtrieben führen müsse, wenn dieselben nicht auch von Hause aus beabsichtigt würden."

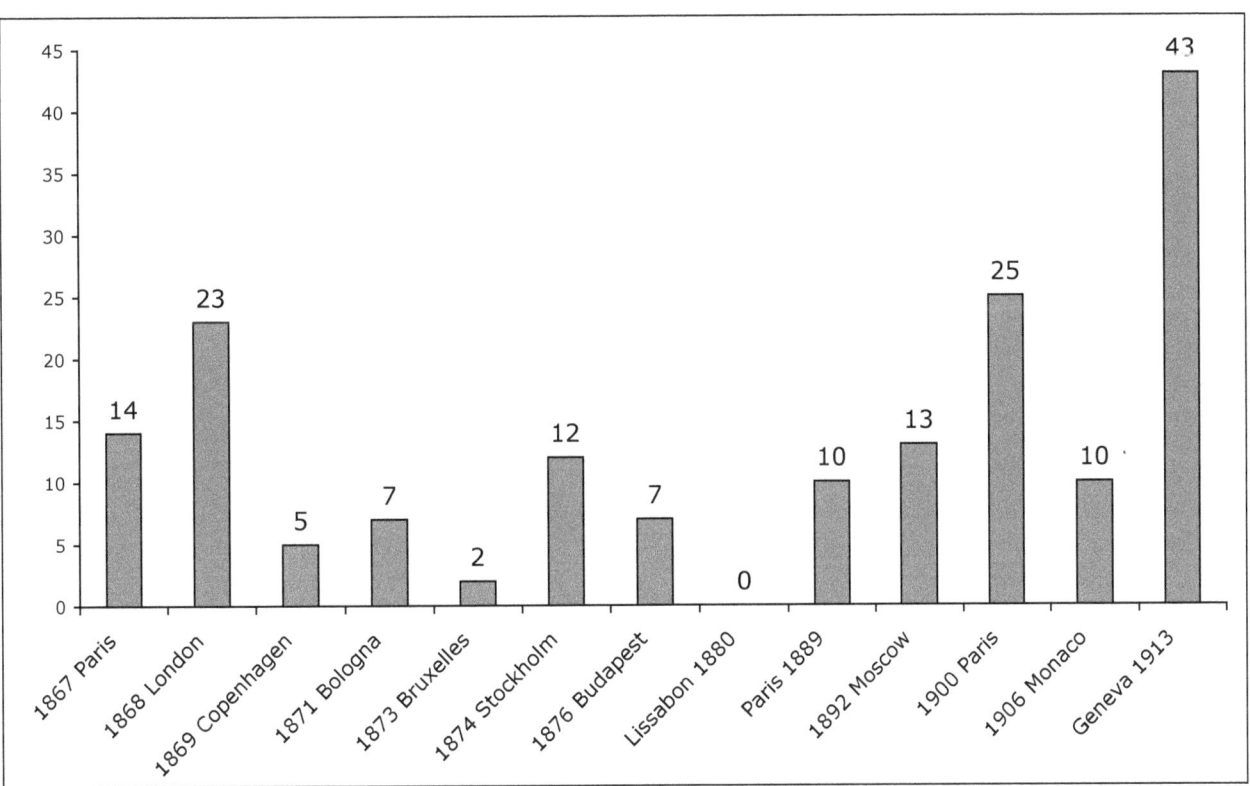

Fig. 4.3. Oversees delegates to CIAAP

After the failed revolution of 1848, finally in 1852 a "Collective Historical Society" (Gesammtverein der deutschen Geschichts- und Alterthumsvereine) was founded, which included a prehistoric section. The new society was greeted with high hopes, but already after two years it became clear that it had effectively failed, due to a lack of funds, lack of support by the diverse German states and increasingly strong disagreements between its members, especially Ludwig Lindenschmit, the director of the Romano-German Museum at Mainz, who regarded it as the only legitimate German national Museum, Freiherr Hans von Aufsessss of the Germanic National Museum at Nuremburg and Friedrich Lisch from Schwerin.[6]

The foundation of the German Society for Anthropology, Ethnology and Prehistory (short DAG or German Anthropological Society) by Virchow in 1869 was clearly spurred by the example of the CIAAP. "The decision of 1869 [to found the DAG] which has indeed led to important consequences, was caused by a series of fundamental changes of view among the scholars of Europe that took place in the preceding decennium which found their visible expression in the foundation of the international prehistoric Conferences [CIAAP]" (Virchow 1894, 80).

The perspective of the DAG was international rather than national. "We aimed at putting in the foundations for an edifice whose walls, not regarding the name, should encompass more than the narrow frame of the German countries... The German name of the society does not tie our members to the soil, their research shall freely encompass the whole globe..." (Virchow 1870a, 1). Virchow deemed that it was impossible to understand German prehistory without recourse to worldwide comparative studies. It was repeatedly emphasised that other nations had overtaken the Germans in the field of anthropological and prehistoric research, and the DAG should "... add a German edifice to the palace already erected by other peoples in a neighbourly way." (ibd.), Virchow was campaigning for a peaceful contest between the Nations and among individuals (ibd., 2).

At the meeting of the DAG in Schwerin one year later, Virchow emphasised how an international recognition of the achievements of the German anthropology was lacking because of competing (inter-German) national interests, making the Germans appear thoroughly underdeveloped in this, "their very own field" (Virchow 1870b: 41). In later articles, he was increasingly emphasising the headstart other nations, especially the French and Swiss had on the Germans in prehistoric research (e. g. Virchow 1893, 74). In the 1880s and 1890s, the perceived advances of other nations was a powerful argument in national discourse, especially in a new nation like Germany that feared for its "place at the sun." Even a decided liberal like Virchow was not immune to those sentiments, or maybe he only used them masterfully. This is difficult to tell, as he certainly was a master of irony (Gummel 1938, 265). Later on,

---

[6] see Pranke 1998 for an account of Lindenschmitt.

unfavourable international comparisons certainly cropped up every time the call for more university chairs and better support for museums and collections was raised (Sommer/Struwe 2006, 35-36).

In the period between its foundation and the turn of the century, the DAG was the most important German prehistoric society, with sometimes over 2000 individual members. Its leading members visited CIAAP regularly. The invitations to the meetings and quite detailed accounts of the Conferences were published in the "Zeitschrift für Ethnologie", the society's main organ (e.g. Virchow 1871, Mestorf 1872, Virchow 1880). For the years from 1874 and 1878, the periodical contains a wonderfully detailed register, listing each reference to CIAAP, even in discussions and proceedings. The Congresses are mentioned quite frequently, mainly in passing to make some point in the interpretation of specific archaeological finds. It is clear that attendance at CIAAP gave the respective scholar added academic kudos and was thus frequently, if casually, referred to.[7] As this was the age before the widespread use of photography, and affordable techniques of reproduction were only slowly coming into their own, only personal examination made comparisons and classification possible. Thus, the description of collections and the sites visited on field trips of CIAAP is often longer than the description of sessions.

CIAAP also gave the German delegates the possibility to discuss new developments without having to consider the opinions of other influential German colleagues. For example, Ludwig Lindenschmit (1809-1893), director of the Mainz Romano-German Central-Museum since 1852, was violently opposed to Thomsen's Three Age System. As numerous conference proceedings show, most scholars felt obligated to make at least a show of respecting Lindenschmit's opinions up to the 1880s. Formulations like: "in short, like they would say in Scandinavia, with all respect to Mr. Lindenschmit, a cemetery of the younger *Iron Age* (my emphasis)..."[8] by Virchow (Verhandlungen der deutschen Gesellschaft für Anthropologie, Gratisbeilage 1872, 73), while demonstrating a certain amount of irony, also illustrates the attempt to avoid open conflict with the vitriolic doyen of patriotic archaeology. In the proceedings of CIAAP, in contrast, the "Scandinavian" terminology is used without any reservations. The conferences thus offered the possibility to bypass certain kinds of national orthodoxy.

CIAAP had a considerable influence on the development German archaeology on a more regional level, that is, in individual German countries as well. In the following, I will look at the example of Hans Bruno Geinitz and the "Society for scientific research Isis" in Dresden in some detail.

NATURWISSCHENSCHAFTLICHE GESELLSCHAFT ISIS AND HANS BRUNO GEINITZ

The Isis, as it is commonly known, was a big scholarly society with a decidedly scientific emphasis. It was founded 1833 in the capital of the Kingdom of Saxony by twelve Dresden citizens as a "Verein zur Beförderung der Naturkunde". It was and was renamed "Naturwissenschaftliche Gesellschaft Isis" in 1835 (Gerabek 2002). The society was open to everybody and was decidedly bourgeois, not dominated by the aristocracy as the local Historical Society and the older polymath societies like the "Oberlausitzische Gesellschaft der Wissenschaften in Görlitz". It also had an impressive number of extralocal and even international members. In 1868, the Isis had 608 members, mainly teachers and civil servants, but comparatively few landowners, members of the military or clerics.

In 1844, specialized sections for botany, zoology, geology and mineralogy were established. Prehistoric subjects were occasionally touched upon in the meetings of the mineralogical and geodesic section. For example, in 1861, Leonhard Horner, President of the London Geological society gave a lecture on "the antiquity of Mankind" that attracted "multiple members of the public" (Sitzungsber. Isis 1860, 3).[9] In 1862, the recent German translation of Darwins "Origin of Species" and "The improbably of the descent of humanity from a common original couple" (Mannheim 1861) by the radical theologian Georg Friedrich Schlatter were discussed and the president concluded that every natural scientist should peruse these important books (Sitzungsber. Isis 1862, 53-54). The Neanderthal finds were discussed in 1865, but presumably not accepted as proof of antediluvian man. Pile-dwellings were the subject of a lecture by Ferdinand von Hochstetter in 1865.

In contrast, local "antediluvian" finds like bones or flints presented by members of the society were normally dismissed in a rather cavalier manner by Hans Bruno Geinitz, the head of the section, who would point out a lack of secure associations or their doubtful artificial character.

Hans Bruno Geinitz (1814-1900) had studied in Berlin and Jena (PhD in 1837) and was a pupil of Friedrich August von Quenstedt (1809–1889), a well-known German geologist and palaeontologist (Encyclo-pedia Britannica 1911). In 1850, Geinitz became the first professor of geology and mineralogy ("Geognosie, Mine-

---

[7] In 1900, Virchow was criticised for visiting too many conferences, After pointing out that he had not visited 39, but only 10 conferences, he went on to emphasise that prehistory was a young discipline, which make the attendance at numerous meetings a necessity (Correspondenzblatt für Anthropologie 32, 1901, 73).

[8] "kurz, wie man in Skandinavien sagen würde, mit Erlaubnis des Hrn. Collegen Lindenschmit, es ist also ein der jüngeren Eisenzeit angehöriges Gräberfeld..."

[9] The proceedings do not make it clear if Horner was really present in person.

ralogie und Naturgeschichte") at the Royal Polytechnic School at Dresden. Since 1857, he was director of the Royal Mineralogical and Geological Museum at Dresden, posts which he held till 1894 (Grunert *et al.* 2001). Geinitz was quite an influential geologist at the time (cf. Sarjeant 1980). Charles Darwin, for example, for revising Heinrich Georg Bronn's translation of his "Origin of species" (Darwin 1859), but Geinitz finally declined (http://darwin.lib.cam.ac.uk). Since 1861, Geinitz had repeatedly been either president of the society or member of the executive council of Isis (Zaunick 1935, 156), and he unopposedly ran the section of geognosy and mineralogy.

In 1867, Geinitz travelled to Paris to attend the extraordinary session of the Geological Society of France that took place from the 5.-12. August 1867. He later wrote an account for the Proceedings of the Isis (Geinitz 1867a). In this year, Paris was the venue of the Second Worldfair. It lasted from the 1st of April to the 3rd of November, attracting about 7 million visitors (Krutisch 2001, 42). In the very centre of the main exhibition hall, there was a display of "The history of work" (Galerie de l'Histoire du travail) that presented prehistoric finds from France and other European countries (Mortillet 1867). The influence of this exhibition on the development of prehistory has always been emphasized (Daniel 1962, Bibby 1956) and recently been closer reviewed by Müller-Scheessel (1999, 2001, 2003).

The exhibition was visited by the delegates of the Geological Society on the 6th of August, and the archaeological exhibition was duly noted by Geinitz in one short paragraph of his account. On the 8th, the geologist's conference visited the "diluvial region" of Paris. They inspected archaeological finds from the gravels ("diluvium gris"), but Geinitz remained doubtful about their age (Geinitz 1867a, 95).

All in all, 14 international conferences took place during the World Fair (Krutisch 2001, 44). Geinitz had presumably travelled to Paris for the Geologist's conference, but he stayed on for the CIAAP, which started a week later (17.-30.8. 1867). He reported his impressions in the following number of the minutes of Isis (Geinitz 1867b). He visited the Prehistoric gallery again on the 18th of August with a delegation from the archaeological conference. This time, Geinitz's description is over four pages long. He gives a short description of some of the artefacts, but his main emphasis is on the chronological scheme underlying the exhibition. In the French section, the finds had been divided into the following periods, according to Geinitz:

1. Era of the reindeer or Quaternary, with crude flint-tools, corresponding to the finds from the Diluvian gravels (*diluvium gris* of the Paris-region). This was the "*premier age de la Pierre*".

2. Era of polished stone "which one might consider to equate with the *Diluvium rouge*" (this seems to be Geinitz' own conclusion)

3. Celtic Era oder earlier Bronze Age, later the first iron tools

4. *Epoque Gauloise* or Iron Age

5. Gallo-Roman Era

6. Merowingian and Carolingian Era

This division of the Stone age is essentially the scheme to be popularised by John Lubbock in his "Prehistoric times" (1865) and extended by J. Worsae, who separated the crude stone tools found in the caves and the drift from those occurring on the coast and in the Køkkenmøddinger (Gräslund 1987, 36-39).

Thomsen's Three-age system was known in Germany at the time, and is referred to in the proceedings of the Isis as the "dominant view" (Sitzungsberichte 1865, 28), but never discussed in detail. The appellation as the "Nordic" Three-age system (ibd.) may indicate that the anonymous reporter followed the influential German archaeologist Ludwig Lindenschmit in rejecting its applicability outside of Scandinavia. But as already mentioned, Geinitz never showed much interest in prehistory before his visit to Paris. I would speculate that the system proposed in Paris made much more sense to him as a geologist than the Three-Age-System, linked, as it was, to geological strata and stratified deposits. It was framed in a language a geologist could understand and make sense of. It was a system that connected "antiquities" and geology. This close connection between archaeology and geology lies at the root of the development of the stratigraphic method, and was a tradition prevalent in France, but not very common in Germany, neither then or later on. Antiquarians had classified finds according to attributes inherent to the artefacts. This was mainly the raw material, as for Thomsen, Danneil and Lisch in different versions of the Three-Age-System for or Büsching (1824) in his independent, now completely forgotten scheme. While Thomsen recorded and took into account the composition of an assemblage, the stratigraphic position was not monitored, while the French system was almost exclusively based on stratigraphic context.

Geinitz also visited the Musée des Antiquités Nationales at St-Germain, and the Somme gravels at Amiens and St-Acheul and inspected the artefacts. He came to the conclusion that these finds left no doubt as to the association of man with extinct animals although he still emphasised that not all deposits were trustworthy and sometimes they contained mixed deposits from different periods.

After Geinitz's return to Dresden, a section for "prehistoric archaeology" (vorhistorische Alterthumskunde) of the Isis was founded in November 1869. The name clearly reflects that of the Congress. The members were quite active and investigated a number of sites, not only of Palaeolithic Age, but others like the urnfields of Strehlen and Grossenhain and the Slavonic hillfort of

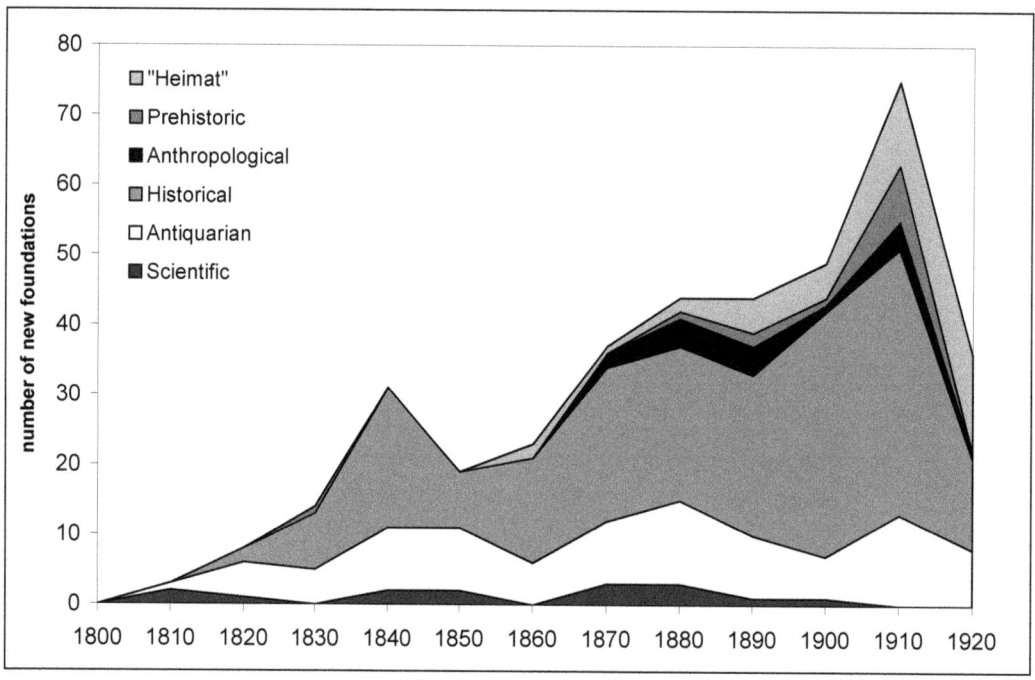

Fig. 4.4. Names of newly founded German societies, 1800-1920

Koschütz near Dresden. In 1869, two new cupboards containing finds demonstrating the co-occurrence of early man and extinct animals were added to the exhibition of the mineralogical Museum at Dresden (Geinitz 1869, 95). Geinitz also got in contact with other scholars interested in early man, like Oscar Fraas in Stuttgart and Emile Cartailhac in France (ibd.). Cartailhac's "Matériaux pour l'histoire primitive et naturelle de l'Homme" were acquired by exchange. The prehistoric collection was to grow dramatically in the following years, and in 1874 an independent "Prehistoric collection" was established.

Geinitz had registered for the London Congress in 1868, but never turned up. Other members of the Isis took part in CIAAP, for example F. Mehwald, the president of the prehistoric section in 1869 in Copenhagen and Ida von Boxberg in Paris 1889. No members of other Saxon societies seem to have been present in Paris 1867, the only other Saxons attending being members of the University of Leipzig, mainly physicians and anatomists.

The example of Geinitz shows how the CIAAP could also be extremely influential on developments in the German states. There is not much evidence of contact between the prehistorians of the Isis and other German antiquarian societies, and almost no contact with the local historical society that was heavily dominated by members of the court and the local aristocracy. But the influence of CIAAP seems to have been restricted to a very narrow timeslot, introducing and promoting the idea of the antiquity of man at a time when this was already a focus of interest for a number of scholars.[10] After this initial simulation, contact seems to have lagged in Geinitz' case,

though he still received publications and probably kept in contact with colleagues through other venues.

This might indeed be the general pattern and a reason for the ultimate demise of the Congresses. In 1897 Virchow stated: "When we (DAG) started, the attention was concentrated on general questions." The origin of man, the age of the reindeer and the mammoth as well as the pile dwellings were at the centre of common interest. "I may remind you of the International Conferences taking place at this time. We did not tire to return to those questions, but now we feel the need to consider questions that concerns us Germans, as opposed to those questions that foreign scholars have to come to grips with." (Correspondenzblatt der deutschen Anthropologischen Gesellschaft 1897, 67). At an earlier date, he had described the German scramble to keep up with the discoveries of the Swiss and the French, to find traces of diluvial man and pile-dwellings. "No lake, no pond, no swampy hole" was overlooked in the search for pile-dwellings. But then genuine cavemen and pile-dwellings had been found, "and as we have become equal to other peoples in this regard, the former restless interest in the discovery of such finds has somewhat abated (Correspondenzblatt der deutschen Anthropologischen Gesellschaft 1893, 74). Now, "here as elsewhere" a national task had become more important: "the first and basic task is to interest our compatriots in the national possessions and to encourage them to research and preserve our native treasures." (Correspondenzblatt der deutschen Anthropologischen Gesellschaft 1897, 67).

As the antiquity of mankind slowly was accepted and prehistoric knowledge in general increased, it became more common to concentrate on local finds entirely, and

---

[10] Hermann Schaffhausen (Bonn) might provide another example.

the construction of local chronologies became the main focus of a new generation of scholars (cf. Sommer and Struwe 2006, 32), like O. Tischler and P. Reinecke in Germany. Increased professionalisation and a growing number of scholars led to the growth of regional and national networks (Sommer 2005). Also, the failure of endeavours like the Commission for prehistoric maps[11] (as opposed to the level of international coordination attained by the anthropologists, the London Craniometric Accord for example) may have reduced the enthusiasm of the prehistorians.

In Germany, the Nationalism of the 1870s changed to increasing chauvinism as the century came to its close. There was also a paradigmatic change in prehistory, from an universalist anthropology that included ethnology and prehistory as well as somatic anthropology to a nationalist Pre-History that strove to find national roots in the deep past with the help of linguistic research, as represented by Gustaf Kossinna (1858-1931). This was a more general trend, as can be shown, for example, by the names of newly founded societies, where "Anthropology" goes out of favour and is replaced by "homeland" (Heimat) and related expressions (fig. 4.4).

In conclusion, the CIAAP had a fundamental importance for the development of German archaeology, even if it never met in the country. But this influence was restricted mainly to the period between 1868 and ca. 1880, when the idea of the antiquity of mankind was still new and fascinating and dominated the international discourse. Once this and the new chronological framework it stood for was accepted, the emphasis of research and scholarly discussions seems to have changed to more local issues.

Bibliography

BIBBY, G. (1956) – The testimony of the spade. New York: A. Knopf

BÜSCHING, G.F. (1824) – Abriß der deutschen Alterthumskunde. Weimar.

CARTAILHAC, E. (1880) – Congrès international d'anthropologie et d'archéologie préhistoriques, Rapport sur la session de Lisbonne. Paris: Eugène Boban.

DANIEL, G. (1962) – The idea of prehistory. Hammondsworth: Penguin.

GEINITZ, H.B. (1867a) – Mittheilungen über die ausserordentliche Versammlung der geologischen Gesellschaften von Frankreich in Paris, am 5. bis 12. August 1867. Sitzungsberichte und Abhandlungen der Naturwissenschaftlichen Gesellschaft Isis Dresden 1867, p. 93-99.

GEINITZ, H.B. (1867b) – Der Internationale Congress für Anthropologie und vorhistorische Archäologie in Paris, 17.-30. August 1867. Sitzungsberichte und Abhandlungen der Naturwissenschaftlichen Gesellschaft Isis Dresden 1867, p. 147-155.

GEINITZ, H.B. (1869) – Mittheilungen aus dem Königl. Mineralogischen Museum in Dresden über das Jahr 1868. Sitzungsberichte und Abhandlungen der Naturwissenschaftlichen Gesellschaft Isis Dresden 1869, p. 95-97.

GERABEK, W.E. (2002) – Die Dresdner "Naturwissenschaftliche Gesellschaft Isis", ein historischer Abriss. In Döring, D; Nowak, K. eds. – Gelehrte Gesellschaften im mitteldeutschen Raum (1650-1820), Teil II. Abhandlungen der Sächsischen Akademie der Wissenschaften zu Leipzig. Philologisch-historische Klasse 76:5. Leipzig: S. Hirzel, p. 169-174.

GRAFTON, A. (1999) – Cardano's cosmos, the worlds and works of a Renaissance-Astrologer. Cambridge: Harvard University Press.

GRÄSLUND, B. (1987) – The birth of prehistoric chronology. Cambridge: Cambridge University Press.

GRUNERT, S.; SCHNEIDER, H.; ULLRICH, B. (2001) – Die geologische Lehr- und Forschungstätigkeit an der Technischen Universität Dresden seit Hans Bruno Geinitz. Abhandlungen des Museums für Mineralogie und Geologie Dresden 46/47, p. 49 – 55.

GUMMEL, H. (1938) – Forschungsgeschichte in Deutschland. Berlin: de Gruyter.

JACOBEIT, W. (1965) – Bäuerliche Wirtschaft und Arbeit. Ein Beitrag zur Wissenschaftsgeschichte der Volkskunde. Veröffentlichungen des Instituts für deutsche Volkskunde 39. Berlin: Akademie.

KOSSACK, G. (1999) – Prähistorische Archäologie in Deutschland im Wandel der geistigen und politischen Situation. Bayer. Akad. Wiss., phil.-hist. Klasse, Sitzungsber. 1999/4. München: Beck.

KRASZEWSKI I.-J. (1874) – Congrès International d'Anthropologie et d'Archéologie préhistoriques. Session de 1874 à Stockholm, notes de Voyage. Paris.

KRUTISCH, P. (2001) – Aus aller Herren Länder. Weltausstellungen seit 1851. Kulturgeschichtliche Spaziergänge im germanischen Nationalmuseum 4. Nürnberg: Germanisches Nationalmuseum.

MEHWALD, F. (1869) – Der eigenthümliche Verlauf des archäologischen Congresses zu Kopenhagen vom 27. August bis 5. September 1869. Sitzungsberichte und Abhandlungen der Naturwissenschaftlichen Gesellschaft Isis Dresden 1869, p. 235-241.

MESTORF, J. (1872) – Der Internationale Congress der Archäologen und Anthropologen in Brüssel 1871. Correspondenzblatt der deutschen Anthropologischen Gesellschaft 3, p. 81-85 and 89-96.

MORTILLET, G. (1867) – Promenades préhistoriques à l'Exposition universelle. Matériaux pour l'histoire positive et philosophique de l'Homme 5-6, p. 181-368.

---

[11] See the contribution of Hurel & Vialet, in this volume.

MORTILLET, G. (1867) – Compte rendu de la reunion à Neuchâtel (Suisse) du Congrés International Paléoethnologique. Matériaux pour l'histoire positive et philosophique de l'Homme 2, p. 469-528.

MORTILLET, G. (1871) – Introduction. Comptes rendus du Congrès International d'Anthropologie et d'Archéologie Préhistoriques 5, Bologna 1871, p. I-XVI.

MÜLLER-SCHEESSEL, N. (1998/99) – Im Schatten des Eifelturms: die Präsentation von Pfahlbauten und Pfahlbaufunden auf Weltausstellungen. Plattform 7/8, 22-31.

MÜLLER-SCHEESSEL, N. (2001) – Fair prehistory: archaeological exhibits at French Expositions universelles. Antiquity 75, p. 391-401.

MÜLLER-SCHEESSEL, N. (2003) – Von der Zeichenhaftigkeit archäologischer Ausstellung und Museen. In: Veit, U. et al. (eds.), Spuren und Botschaften: Interpretationen materieller Kultur. Münster: Waxmann, p. 107-126.

MÜLLER-SCHEESSEL, N. (in press) – "...Dem Romanismus entgegentreten", National animosities amoung the participants of the Congrès international d'anthropologie et d'archéologie préhistoriques. In Gramsch, A. and U. Sommer (eds.), German Archaeological Theory and Practice in its European context (UPAS, Bonn).

PRANKE, T. (1998) – Altertumskunde zwischen Fortschritt und Beharrung. Ludwig Lindenschmit d. Ä. (1808-1893) in seiner Zeit. Jahrbuch des Römisch-Germanischen Zentralmuseums Mainz 45:2, p. 711-774.

SARJEANT, W.A.S. (1980) – Geologists and the history of geology: an international bibliography from the origins to 1978. London: Macmillan.

SOMMER, U. (2005) – Vorgeschichtsforschung in der Frühzeit des Verbandes. Archäologisches Nachrichtenblatt 10:4, p. 367-383.

SOMMER, U.; STRUWE, R. (2006) – Bemerkungen zur prähistorischen Archäologie an deutschen Universitäten im 19. Jahrhundert. In Callmer, J. et al. eds. – Die Anfänge der vor- und frühgeschichtlichen Archäologie als akademisches Fach (1890-1930) im europäischen Vergleich. Internationale Tagung an der Humboldt-Universität zu Berlin vom 13.-16. März 2003. Rahden (Westfalen):Leidorf, p. 23-42.

PREHISTORIA 2000 – Revue de l'Union Internationale des Sciences Préhistoriques et Protohistoriques. 1, 2000, Liege.

VIRCHOW, R. (1870a) – Die deutsche Gesellschaft für Anthropologie, Ethnologie und Urgeschichte. Correspondenzblatt der deutschen Gesellschaft für Anthropologie, Ethnologie und Urgeschichte 1, p. 1-2.

VIRCHOW, R. (1870b) – Eröffnungsrede zur 2. allgemeinen Versammlung der deutschen anthropologischen Versammlung zu Schwerin. Correspondenzblatt der deutschen Gesellschaft für Anthropologie, Ethnologie und Urgeschichte 6-10, p. 41-47.

VIRCHOW, R. (1871) – Über die anthropologischen Versammlungen zu Schwerin und Bologna. Zeitschrift für Ethnologie 3, p. 137-144.

VIRCHOW, R. (1880) – Der Internationale prähistorische Congress in Lissabon. Zeitschrift für Ethnologie (Verhandlungen DAG), p. 333-355.

VIRCHOW, R. (1893) – Die heutigen Probleme der anthropologischen Forschung. Correspondenzblatt der deutschen Gesellschaft für Anthropologie, Ethnologie und Urgeschichte 24, p. 74-79.

VIRCHOW, R. (1894) – Eröffnungsrede. Correspondenzblatt der deutschen Gesellschaft für Anthropologie, Ethnologie und Urgeschichte, p. 80-87.

WIELL, S. (1999) – The Congress of Anthropology and Archaeology in Copenhagen 1869 – Behind the stage. Antiquity 73, p. 136-142.

ZAUNICK, R. (1935) – Hans Bruno Geinitz (1814-1900). Sitzungsberichte Naturforschende Gesellschaft Isis, p. 156-158.

The Darwin Correspondence Online Database, (http://darwin.lib.cam.ac.uk), accessed 01/10/2006.

Tab. 4.2. German delegates at CIAAP

Name	First Name	Titel	occupation	Residence	La Spezia	Neuchâtel	Paris 1867	Paris 1867 Correspondants	London 1868, correspondants	Copenhagen 1869	Bologna 1871	Brussel 1873 correspondants	Bruxelles Membres	Stockholm 1874 Korrespondants	Stockholm membres	Budapest 1876	Lissabonn 1880	Moskau 1892	Paris 1889 Membres	Paris 1889 correspondants	Paris 1900	Paris 1900 membres	Monaco 1906	Genf 1912
Abegg		Dr.	Directeur de la maternité	Danzig												1	1	1						
Abegg	W.	Dr.	bank manager	Berlin												1								
Abegg	J.	Mle		Wiesbaden												1								
Ahles		Prof.		Stuttgart								1												
Andree	Richard	Dr.		Leipzig															1	1				
Arnold	Jules	Prof.		Heidelberg								1												
Arzruni	A.	Prof.	Prof.	Aachen														1						
Ascherson	T.	Prof.	Member of the Academy of Sciences	Berlin												1								
Auerbach	Richard			Berlin																	1	1		
aus'm Weerth		Prof.		Kessenich bei Bonn								1	1											
Baier	B.		librarian	Stralsund								1	1											
Bartels		Dr.		Braunschweig-Neustrelitz													1							
Bartels	Max	Dr.	Musée Ethnographique	Berlin													1	1	1	1				
Bastian		Dr. phil.	Director of the Ethnographic Museum, Berlin	Berlin					1			1		1	1		1	1	1					
Behrendt		Mde		Berlin																			1	
Beltz	Robert	Dr.	Dr., conservateur du Musée Grand-Ducal de Schwerin	Schwerin																	1	1		
Berchem	M.	Graf	Ministre à Madrid												1									
Berendt		Prof.		Königsberg											1									
Bergau	R.	Prof.		Königsberg											1									
Bernett		Dr.		Berlin																			1	
Bieberstein		Mde		Berlin																			1	
Birkner		Dr.		München																			1	
Blasius	Wilhelm	Dr.		Braunschweig													1							
Blume				Bonn											1									
Boch	Eugen		manufacturier	Saarburg			1																	
Braun	Alexander	Prof.		Berlin								1												
Brinkmann	J.	Prof.		Hamburg								1												
Buchner	Louis	Prof.		Darmstadt								1												
Buschan	Georg	Dr.	médecin de la marine Imperiale	Wilhelmshaven														1						
Carus	J. V.	Prof.		Leipzig								1	1											
Christ	W.	Dr. phil.	Professeur de l'Universite	München						1		1	1											
Cumano		Dr.		Cormons						1														
Dahn	Felix	Prof.													1									
Dalmann	Gustav	Dr. theol	Directeur de l'institut évangélique allemand pour la science de l'antiqiuté de la Terre Sainte Jerusalem	Jerusalem																				1
de Sczaniecki	Michel		Membre de la Société des Sciences de Thorn	Navra, bei Culmsee													1							
Deichmüller		Dr.	Conservateur de Musée Préhistorique	Dresden																	1	1		
Dieffenbach	Lorenz			Frankfurt/M				1																
Diercks	Gustav	Dr.		Dresden													1							
Dillenius	Julienne	Dr.		München																				1
Dohrn	Anton	Dr.	Jena university	Jena						1														
Drawe				Suskozin/Danzig												1	1							
Duboc				Dresden												1								
d'Uexküll		Baron		Coburg												1								
Dumont		Dr.		Berlin								1	1											
Ebert		Prof.		Leipzig								1	1											
Ecker	Alexander	Dr.	Professeur d'anatomie a l'Universite de Fribourg (Breisgau)	Freiburg	1	1	1					1	1											
Esselen		Dr.	privy councellor	Hamm								1	1											
Essenwein			Director of the Germanic National Museum, Nuremburg	Nürnberg								1					1							

Archaeologists without boundaries: Towards a history of international archaeological congresses (1866-2006)

Name	First Name	Titel	occupation	Residence	La Spezia	Neuchâtel	Paris 1867	Paris 1867 Correspondants	London 1868, correspondants	Copenhagen 1869	Bologna 1871	Brussel 1873 correspondants	Bruxelles Membres	Stockholm 1874 Korrespondants	Stockholm membres	Budapest 1876	Lissabonn 1880	Moskau 1892	Paris 1889 correspondants	Paris 1889 Membres	Paris 1900	Paris 1900 membres	Monaco 1906	Genf 1912
Ewald		Dr.	Director of the Museum for applied arts, Berlin	Berlin								1			1					1				
Faudel	M. M.	Dr.		Colmar																1				
Feltmanovksy	Jérome		Directeur Musée d'Archéologie	Posen												1								
Finsch	Otto		Explorateur	Bremen																1				
Forrer	Robert	Dr.	Conservateur des antiquités préhistoriques et romanes, Musée Strasbourg	Straßburg																				1
Förstemann	E.	Dr.	Director of the Royal library, Dresden	Dresden										1	1									
Forster	E.	Dr.		München								1												
Fraas	Otto	Dr.	Directeur du musée geologique de Stuttgart	Stuttgart	1		1	1	1			1	1	1	1					1				
Friedel	E.			Berlin											1									
Friedenthal																							1	
Fritsch	G.	Dr.		Berlin											1					1				
Fuhlrott		Prof.		Elberfeld				1	1			1			1					1				
Geinitz	Hans Bruno	Prof.	Professeur a Dresde	Dresden			1	1	1			1			1					1				
Genthe	H.	Prof.		Frankfurt/M										1	1									
Gentz	W.		Paintre-artiste	Berlin											1									
Gerlach		Dr.		Erlangen								1												
Gerland	G.	Dr.		Halle											1									
Gerland		Prof.		Straßburg																1				
Götz		Dr.															1							
Grad	Charles		Deputé																	1				
Graf	Engelbert		Ecrivain	Berlin																				1
Grempler	Wilhelm	Dr.	Médécin	Breslau											1			1		1	1			
Griesinger		Prof.		Berlin			1																	
Grotefend		Dr.	Directeur des archives	Hannover								1			1									
Gumbel	W.	Dr.		München								1												
Haak		Prof.	Directeur du musée d'archéologie à Stuttgart	Stuttgart								1												
Haake		Dr. med.		Braunschweig																				1
Hahne	Hans	Dr.		Berlin																			1	
Handelmann		Prof.	Museum Director	Kiel								1	1	1	1	1	1			1	1			
Handelmann		Madame		Kiel												1								
Hartmann	Auguste	Prof.	Attaché a Bibliotheque Royale	München								1		1	1	1				1				
Hasskarl		Dr.		Cleve											1									
Hassler		Prof. Dr.		Ulm								1												
Helm	O.		Pharmacien	Danzig												1	1							
Helmholtz	H.	Prof.	Professeur a la Universite de Heidelberg	Heidelberg				1																
Hesse, geb. Herwarth	C.	Mne		Bonn													1							
His		Prof.		Leipzig											1					1	1			
Hostmann		Dr.		Celle						1		1			1									
Hrasewski	Joseph Ignatz			Dresden							1													
Jacobs		Dr.		München																			1	
Jagor	F.	Dr. phil.		Berlin				1						1	1					1	1			
Jeitteles				Olmütz					1															
Jentzsch	C.-A.	Dr.		Leipzig											1									
Joest	W.	Dr.		Berlin																	1			
Jöst	E.			Köln																	1			
Kessler	Fritz			Sulzmatt																			1	1
Kiepers		Prof.		Berlin								1												
Kiepert		Prof.		Berlin											1					1				
Klaatsch	Hermann	Prof. Dr.	Prof., Institut anatomique	Heidelberg																		1		
Klemm									1															
Klopffleisch		Dr.		Jena								1			1					1				

Name	First Name	Titel	occupation	Residence	La Spezia	Neuchâtel	Paris 1867	Paris 1867 Correspondants	London 1868, correspondants	Copenhagen 1869	Bologna 1871	Brussel 1873 correspondants	Bruxelles Membres	Stockholm 1874 Korrespondants	Stockholm membres	Budapest 1876	Lissabonn 1880	Moskau 1892	Paris 1889 correspondants	Paris 1889 Membres	Paris 1900	Paris 1900 membres	Monaco 1906	Genf 1912
Klug	K.	Dr.		Lübeck							1	1												
Knorr	Friedrich	Dr.	Museum of Patriotic Antiqities	Kiel																			1	1
Kollmann	Jules	Prof.	Professor for Anatomy, University Basel	München							1		1	1	1								1	
Koner		Prof. Dr.		Berlin							1	1												
Konried			Principauté	Monaco																			1	
Körner		Dr.		Berlin																			1	
Kraszewski	J.-I.			Dresden										1										
Kraus		Prof.		Hannover						1														
Krause	Eduard		Conservateur de Musée Royal d'Ethnographie	Berlin															1	1		1		
Krug von Nida			Directeur des Mines et des Forges	Berlin							1													
Kühne	Max	Dr.		Berlin										1	1		1	1						
Künne	Charles		Membre Societé Anthropologique	Berlin										1	1		1		1					
Kurtz	Frédéric	can phil		Berlin											1									
Küster	E.	Dr.		Berlin											1									
Küster	Marie	Mde		Berlin											1									
Lachmann	Th.			Ueberlingen					1															
Lallmant	R.		Médécin	Lübeck										1										
Langerhans	Paul	Dr.		Freiburg										1			1		1					
Lazarus		Prof. Dr.		Berlin							1	1							1					
Lepsius	B.	Prof.	Directeur de la bibliotèque royale	Berlin							1	1												
Leuckart	R.	Prof.		Leipzig							1	1												
Lexow	C.-V.		Consul	Lübeck										1										
Lindenschmitt	Ludwig	Dr.	Directeur du Musee de Mayence	Darmstadt			1	1			1	1							1					
Lisch	Friedrich	Dr	Avocat, Directuer du Musee et des Archives de Schwerin	Schwerin	1		1	1	1		1	1												
Lissauer		Dr.	Bibliotecaire Societé Anthropologique	Danzig										1	1		1		1		1	1		
Lissauer		Mde		Berlin																		1		
Lucae		Prof. Dr.		Frankfurt			1	1			1	1												
Luchs	H.	Dr.	Conservateur du musée d'archéologie Breslau	Breslau										1										
Maas				Hamburg							1													
Malbranche				Würzburg													1							
Mannhardt	W.	Dr.		Danzig										1	1									
Martin	R.																				1	1		
Masch			Directeur des Archives, curé	Demmern										1	1									
Maurer	Konrad	Prof.		München										1										
Mehwald		Dr.		Dresden							1	1		1	1									
Merkel	F.	Dr.		Göttingen								1												
Mestorf	J.	Mademoiselle	Conservateur du musée Archéologique	Kiel						1	1	1	1	1	1	1	1		1	1	1			
Metzdorf	Max		Musée d'Antiquités	Kiel												1								
Meyer	A.-B.		Royal ethnographic Museum, Dresden	Dresden															1					
Michelsen	Th.			Schwerin																			1	
Mieg	Matthieu			Mühlhausen																			1	
Milde			Artiste, paintre	Lübeck							1													
Miller			Conseiller d'Etudes	Hannover							1													
Morlot						1																		
Müllenhoff		Prof. Dr.		Berlin							1	1												
Müller		Dr.	Directeur du Musée d'archéologie à Hannovre	Hannover										1										
Münsterberg	M.			Danzig													1							
Naue	Julius			Stuttgart																1				
Nehring		Prof.	Ecole vetérinaire	Berlin																1				
Nöggerath		Prof.	Directeur des Mines	Bonn						1				1										
Obst		Dr.		Leipzig										1										
Oehlschläger			Médécin	Danzig											1									

ARCHAEOLOGISTS WITHOUT BOUNDARIES: TOWARDS A HISTORY OF INTERNATIONAL ARCHAEOLOGICAL CONGRESSES (1866-2006)

Name	First Name	Titel	occupation	Residence	La Spezia	Neuchâtel	Paris 1867	Paris 1867 Correspondants	London 1868, correspondants	Copenhagen 1869	Bologna 1871	Brussel 1873 correspondants	Bruxelles Membres	Stockholm 1874 Korrespondants	Stockholm membres	Budapest 1876	Lissabonn 1880	Moskau 1892	Paris 1889 correspondants	Paris 1889 Membres	Paris 1900	Paris 1900 membres	Monaco 1906	Genf 1912
Ohlshausen	Otto	Dr.		Berlin																1				
Paetsch	I.			Berlin													1							
Paetsch	I.		Médécin	Berlin													1							
Pagenstecher	A.	Prof.	Université Heidelberg	Heidelberg							1													
Peschel	O.	Prof.		Leipzig							1		1											
Petermann	A.	Dr.		Gotha							1		1		1									
Petermann		Mde		Berlin											1									
Petersen	Christian	Bibliotecaire		Hamburg						1	1													
Pinder		Dr.	Directeur du Musée de Cassel	Kassel											1									
Plessner		Dr.		Berlin																1				
Priber			avocat	Frankenberg											1									
Prüner-Bey		Dr.					1						1	1										
Quenstedt		Prof.		Tübingen							1													
Rademacher				Köln																				1
Ranke	Johannes	Prof. Dr.		München															1					1
Rauber				Leipzig															1					
Rehlen	W.			Nürnberg																				1
Reichert		Prof.		Berlin							1													
Reiss	W.	Dr.		Berlin															1	1				
Reiss	Eugene			Berlin																				1
Richter	Eberhard	Prof.		Dresden				1																
Römer		Prof.		Breslau										1										
Rüdiger		Prof.		München										1										
Sandberger		Prof.		Würzburg							1		1											
Schaaffhausen	Henri	Dr./privy Consellor	Professor University Bonn	Bonn			1	1	1	1	1	1	1	1	1	1	1		1	1				
Schaaffhausen	Marie	Mlle		Bonn	1								1		1	1								
Schaaffhausen	Anne	Mlle		Bonn											1	1								
Schaaffhausen	Elisabeth	Mlle		Bonn											1									
Scherzer		Dr.	Anthropologiste de Novarra	Wien					1															
Schemann	Ludwig			Freiburg																				1
Schetelig		Dr. phil.		Holstein						1														
Schierenberg	G.-A.-B.			Meinberg bei Detmold												1								
Schlagintweit	Hermann	Baron		Schloß Jägersburg bei Forchheim			1																	
Schliemann	Heinrich			Athen															1	1				
Schliz	Adolph	Dr.		Heilbronn																			1	
Schmidt	Emil	Dr.	Professeur d'anthropologie à l'université	Leipzig															1	1				
Schoelank	Wilhelm		consul général	Berlin																1				
Schoetensack	Otto	Dr.		Heidelberg																	1	1	1	
Schulz	F.			Boossen, Frankfurt/O												1								
Schulz-Boossen				Boossen, Frankfurt/O												1								
Schuster	Otto		Chapitain des chasseurs	Freiberg							1													
Schwalbe	Gustav	Prof. Dr.	Professor at University	Straßburg																1				1
Schweinfurth	Gustav	Dr.		Berlin														1						
Schurgast		Mme		Berlin																				1
Seler	Eduard			Berlin															1	1		1		
Selenka		Mme		München																				1
Semper		Prof.		Würzburg							1		1				1							
Steimmig	R.		Ingenieur	Danzig											1									
Stein	Albert			Bonn													1							
Steinthal		Prof. Dr.		Berlin								1	1											
Stephan	M.			Frankenberg												1								

Name	First Name	Titel	occupation	Residence	La Spezia	Neuchâtel	Paris 1867	Paris 1867 Correspondants	London 1868, correspondants	Copenhagen 1869	Bologna 1871	Brussel 1873 correspondants	Bruxelles Membres	Stockholm 1874 Korrespondants	Stockholm membres	Budapest 1876	Lissabon 1880	Moskau 1892	Paris 1889 correspondants	Paris 1889 Membres	Paris 1900	Paris 1900 membres	Monaco 1906	Genf 1912
Steudel	Albert	Prof.	Pastor	Ravensburg			1			1	1	1							1					
Stieda	Ludwig	Dr.	Institut anatomique	Königsberg														1		1			1	1
Stoy	Volkmar	Dr. phil.	Professeur a l'Université de Heidelberg	Heidelberg			1																	
Strebel	H.		Voyageur	Hamburg															1					
Stübel	A.	Dr.		Dresden															1	1				
Stuttgärdter	S.		Ingenieur	München											1									
Theobald		Dr.		Hamburg											1									
Tischler	Otto		Secretair de societé physico-économique, Directeur Königsberg	Königsberg												1	1		1	1				
Uhle			Curator at the museum of ethnography	Berlin															1	1				
Unger		Prof.		Wien				1																
Urich			Rentier							1														
Urich		Mde								1														
Urech	Friedrich		Tübingen	Tübingen																				1
Virchow	Rudolf	Dr.	Professor of Medicin	Berlin			1	1	1	1	1	1	1	1	1	1	1	1	1	-	1	1	1	
Virchow	Hans		Institut anatomique	Berlin												1								
von Ahrenberg		Prinz													1									
von Andrian	F.			Aussee															1					
von Asche		Baron		Berlin																			1	
von Asche		Mde		Berlin																			1	
von Asche		Mle		Berlin																			1	
von Biberstein		Mde	Ecriviste	Berlin																				1
von Bibra		Baron		Nürnberg											1									
von Bischoff	L. W.	Prof.		München										1	1									
von Boxberg	Ida	Mle		Schloß Zschorna bei Radeburg															1	1				
von Cohausen	Dr.	Dr., Colonel	Directeur du musée d'antiquités de Wiesbade	Wiesbaden										1	1									
von Dechen		Dr., Geheimrat	President de la Societé d'Histoire naturelle des provinces Rhenanes et de Westpahlie	Bonn										1	1									
von den Steinen	Carl		Voyageur	Berlin															1				1	
von der Marck		Dr.		Hamm											1									
von Donimirski	A.	Dr.		Thorn											1									
von Dücker		Baron	Ingenieur des Mines	Fürstenwalde/Neurode (Schlesien)/Cassel			1			1	1	1	1	1	1		1							
von Eichmann			Ministre a Stockholm												1									
von Estorff	J. O. C.	Baron	Chambelain	Hannover									1	1										
von Eye			Directeur	Nürnberg											1									
von Frantzius		Dr.		Heidelberg									1	1										
von Göppert	H.-R.	Prof., Geheimrat	Professeur, vice-president de la Societé pour les antiques historiques	Breslau			1						1	1										
von Guppenbach		Baron		Puerbach																			1	
von Hefner-Alteneck	J.	Prof.	Directeur du musée historique	München										1	1									
von Hellwald	Friedrich	Baron	Editor of the journal Ausland	Cannstatt										1					1					
von Heydebrand und von der Lasa			Ministre de la confederation de l'Allemagne Du Nord á Copenhagen							1														
von Hölder		Dr., Geheimrat	Conseiller superior de médicine	Stuttgart										1	1									
von Jhering		Dr.		Leipzig											1									
von Landau		Baron		Berlin																			1	
von Lebedur		Dr.	Directeur du musée d'Archéologie Berlin	Berlin									1	1										
von Luschan	Felix	Prof.	Privy counsellor, Ethnographic Museum Berlin	Berlin																1				1

ARCHAEOLOGISTS WITHOUT BOUNDARIES: TOWARDS A HISTORY OF INTERNATIONAL ARCHAEOLOGICAL CONGRESSES (1866-2006)

Name	First Name	Titel	occupation	Residence	La Spezia	Neuchâtel	Paris 1867	Paris 1867 Correspondants	London 1868, correspondants	Copenhagen 1869	Bologna 1871	Brussel 1873 correspondants	Bruxelles Membres	Stockholm 1874 Korrespondants	Stockholm membres	Budapest 1876	Lissabom 1880	Moskau 1892	Paris 1889 correspondants	Paris 1889 Membres	Paris 1900	Paris 1900 membres	Monaco 1906	Genf 1912
von Luschka		Prof.		Tübingen								1	1						1				1	
von Martius	C. F.	Prof.		München				1																
von Prollius	M.			Schwerin											1									
von Quast		Geheimer Rath	Conservateur générale des monuments historiques de la Prusse	Radensleben								1		1	1									
von Sacken		Baron	Musée d'Antiquités	Wien				1																
von Sierakowski	A.	Graf		Waplitz/Altmark										1										
von Wereczynski	P.	Graf												1										
von Wilmowski			Chanonine	Trier								1												
von Wittich		Prof. Dr.		Königsberg								1	1											
Vorwerg	Oskar		Captain	Warmbrunn																				1
Voss	Albert	Dr.	Conservateur du Musée d'Ethnologie	Berlin												1			1	1	1	1		
Wagber				Karlsruhe													1							
Wagner	Moritz	Dr./Pr.		München			1	1	1			1	1	1										
Waldeyer		Prof. Dr.		Berlin															1	1			1	
Wattenbach	W.	Prof.		Berlin										1										
Weber	Ludwig			Berlin																			1	
Weber		Mde		Berlin																			1	
Weinhold	K.	Prof.		Kiel								1	1											
Wekbeker	J.			Düsseldorf													1							
Welcker		Prof.		Halle			1	1						1										
Wesiersky	Aubin Belina	Graf	Membre de la chambre des Seigneurs de Prusse	Pudewicz								1	1	1										
Wibel	Ferdinand	Dr.		Hamburg								1	1											
Wilser	Ludwig	Dr. Médecin		Heidelberg																	1	1		
Wirth	A.	Dr.		München													1						1	
Wörner	L.	Dr.		Darmstadt										1										
Zech	P.	Prof.		Stuttgart								1												
Zenker	W.	Dr.	Directeur de service sanitaire	Frauendorf bei Stettin																	1	1		
Zittel	K	Prof.		München								1		1	1				1					
Museum für Völkerkunde, Hamburg				Hamburg																				1
Kaiserliche Universität und Landesbibliothek Strasbourg				Straßburg																				1
Tübingen, Universitätsbibliothek				Tübingen																				1
Soc. Industrielle				Mühlhausen																			1	
Societé Anthropologique				München																			1	

LES CONGRES INTERNATIONAUX D'ANTHROPOLOGIE ET D'ARCHEOLOGIE PREHISTORIQUES (1866-1912) ET LA QUESTION DE L'EVEIL D'UNE CONSCIENCE PATRIMONIALE COLLECTIVE (FOUILLES, GISEMENTS, COLLECTIONS)

Arnaud HUREL & Amélie VIALET

Département de préhistoire du Muséum national d'histoire naturelle, UMR 5198 du CNRS,
Institut de paléontologie humaine, 1 rue René Panhard, 75013 Paris

Abstract: The "Congrès internationaux d'anthropologie et d'archéologie préhistoriques" take a specific position in the institutionalization process of prehistoric research. They brought to the community of the prehistorians the first permanent scientific structure. These sessions allowed to define then to unify a whole analytical and methodological corpus. Until the congress of Geneva (1912), the internationalist ideal of prehistoric studies is an important vector. The first years of foundation (1866-1880) played a prominent part to radical intellectual conceptions. Then succeeded the years of credibility and legitimacy. But, in both phases, each of the congresses graneds only a marginal position to patrimonial questions – that is, to the idea of a protection of scientific and universal rights to come.
This attitude asks very directly epistemologic questions about the ways of scientific representation in prehistory (what places are recognized to objects and to sites? Does the field of the prehistoric knowledge amount to the immaterial?), about the essence of the prehistorians' activity (does their freedom take precedence over the future of this patrimony?), or the international congresses (why were they not able to bring to the foreground such a patrimonial problem?).
Keywords: Excavations – collections – archaeological awareness – regulation – french exception

Résumé: Les Congrès internationaux d'anthropologie et d'archéologie préhistoriques (IAAP) occupent une place spécifique dans le processus d'institutionnalisation des recherches préhistoriques. Ils ont apporté à la communauté des préhistoriens la première structure scientifique permanente. Ces sessions ont permis de définir puis d'unifier tout un corpus analytique et méthodologique.
Jusqu'au congrès de Genève (1912), l'idéal internationaliste des études préhistoriques est un moteur essentiel. Aux premières années de fondation (1866-1880), marquées par des élaborations conceptuelles radicales, ont succédé les années de crédibilité et de légitimité. Mais, dans ces deux phases, chacune des sessions IAAP ne concède qu'une place marginale aux questions patrimoniales, c'est-à-dire à l'idée de droits scientifiques et universels à venir et à préserver.
Cette attitude pose très directement des questions d'ordre épistémologique sur la nature et les voies de la représentation scientifique en Préhistoire (quelles places sont reconnues aux objets et aux gisements? le champ de la connaissance préhistorique se résume-t-il à l'immatériel?), sur l'essence de l'activité des préhistoriens (leur liberté de fouilleur et de collectionneur doit-elle primer sur le devenir de ce patrimoine?) ou sur les congrès internationaux eux-mêmes (pourquoi n'ont-ils pas pu faire émerger une telle problématique patrimoniale?).
Mots-clé: Fouilles – collections – conscience archéologique – réglementation – exception française

Les Congrès internationaux d'anthropologie et d'archéologie préhistoriques (CIAAP) occupent une place spécifique dans le processus d'institutionnalisation des recherches préhistoriques. À partir de 1866, ils représentent pour la communauté des préhistoriens la première structure scientifique permanente et le lieu de la synthèse des connaissances. Effectivement, grâce à cette primauté structurelle et parce que ces sciences se fondent sur un développement empirique, ces sessions ont permis de définir puis d'unifier tout un corpus intellectuel analytique, terminologique et méthodologique.

Si pour l'historien, "l'histoire se fait avec des documents", la science du préhistorien se fonde, elle aussi, sur des documents objectifs qui sont le gisement et les pièces mises au jour. Il nous semble donc intéressant d'étudier, à travers les sessions des CIAAP, la place accordée à ces éléments en tant qu'objets de science mais aussi en tant que patrimoine indivis qui, de ce point de vue, peut être considéré comme porteur *a priori* de l'idéal communautaire incarné par les CIAAP.

LES CONGRES A LA RECHERCHE D'ELEMENTS FEDERATEURS

À l'image des autres congrès scientifiques internationaux, les CIAAP se sont construits autour d'un idéal internationaliste fondé sur une science "neutralisée", c'est-à-dire "dans un horizon placé au-dessus des agitations politiques et des dissentiments possibles entre gouvernements" (Lartet, 1868, 421). Mais leur caractéristique spécifique est d'avoir été, et d'être perçus par les acteurs eux-mêmes, comme un vecteur essentiel de l'institutionnalisation d'un champ scientifique émergent, qui fait que "l'organisation de l'archéologie préhistorique est en partie l'œuvre des premiers Congrès." (Hubert, 1900, 221). Ce sont ces éléments qu'exprime l'acte de fondation rédigé lors de la réunion extraordinaire de la Spezia en septembre 1865: 1° importance "des études qui ont pour but de nous faire connaître l'origine de l'humanité et les premières pages de l'histoire" et la "nécessité de leur imprimer une bonne direction", 2° "l'immense avantage qui résulte pour la science du rapprochement entre eux de tous les hommes qui s'occupent des recherches antéhistoriques" (*Congrès*, 1868, 2).

De fait, les sessions de Neuchâtel (1866), Paris (1867), Londres (1866), Copenhague (1869), Bologne (1871), Bruxelles (1872), Stockholm (1874), Budapest (1876), Lisbonne (1880), Paris (1889) et Moscou (1892) correspondent à la "période de la lutte et du combat" (Vogt, 1867, 58). La conjonction de l'anthropologie et de l'archéologie préhistoriques permit la réunion de scientifiques de spécialités très différentes. Elle accrut d'autant la conscience identitaire d'une communauté savante jeune et la cohérence d'une science en construction. Elle offrit aux chercheurs français à la fois un lieu d'apprentissage, en l'absence d'enseignement universitaire de ce type et d'une structure nationale pérenne d'échange.[1] Pendant cette période, chaque congrès est l'occasion d'enregistrer des avancées décisives au niveau conventionnel, comme en matière de terminologie ou de classification par exemple, ou sur des débats d'orientation, comme la question de la chronologie ou celle de l'homme tertiaire et de son industrie éolithique.

Mais, dès la session de Moscou, certains s'interrogent sur la feuille de route à confier désormais aux CIAAP. Rudolf Virchow regrette que les débats se limitent "à la classification des objets connus" et que l'archéologie dépossède "de plus en plus l'anthropologie" dont les trouvailles sont rares et contestées (Virchow, 1892, 224). À Paris, en 1900, René Verneau promet un avenir riche de découvertes mais constate que "de grands problèmes archéologiques ont reçu à l'heure actuelle une solution que nous sommes en droit de regarder comme définitive." (Verneau, 1902, 7) Aux premiers congrès, qui furent "les premiers conciles de l'archéologie préhistorique, ceux qui lui dictèrent ses symboles et ses credos" (Hubert, 1900, 223), on oppose le relatif échec de celui de Paris (1900), son "inutilité comme organe scientifique spécial" (*Ibid.*, 228), dans la mesure où il apparaît moins innovant et apporte le constat, en rupture avec l'idéal internationaliste, que se construisent des "églises locales" dont les "conciles nationaux et [les] assemblées régulières suffisent à ses besoins" (*Ibid.*, 223).

De fait, ce deuxième temps, qui s'ouvre à Paris, n'est plus celui des grandes synthèses. Il insère les CIAAP dans le processus logique de normalisation et de spécialisation des débats que tous les congrès scientifiques ont connu, quel que soit le domaine de recherche (Rasmussen, 1995). Au début du XXe siècle, la quasi-totalité des disciplines s'inscrit dans une démarche critique à l'égard des congrès internationaux, doutant même de leur utilité scientifique (perte de leur substance par l'échec du mythe d'une science sans frontières, inflation du nombre des communications, extrême diversité des sujets abordés, spécialisation croissante des chercheurs). Les scientifiques, à la recherche d'un nouvel élan internationaliste, demandent alors aux congrès de se tourner vers les questions d'actualité et de revenir à des thèmes fédérateurs essentiellement normatifs, comme la terminologie ou l'unification des méthodes.

Ainsi, après les temps héroïques de la lutte pour la légitimité et la crédibilité scientifiques, cette nouvelle phase (1900 à 1912) est marquée par l'absence de communications réellement pionnières d'un point de vue conceptuel. Reconnue par tous, la Préhistoire abandonne dans les sessions CIAAP les grands débats d'orientation d'un savoir en construction pour l'échange et l'accommodement particulier au gré des découvertes, l'utopie internationaliste au profit des grands équilibres de pouvoir entre les nations. Les CIAAP rejoignent le commun des congrès internationaux.

L'intérêt croissant pour les questions de cartographie illustre ce mouvement. En 1871, à Bologne, lors de la 5e session, des archéologues soumettent une communication sur les légendes des cartes (Przeziecki, 1873). Une commission internationale est mise en place mais ne se réunit pas, en raison du décès de son initiateur, Alexandre Przezdziecki. En 1874, à Stockholm, Ernest Chantre présente un rapport sur le projet d'une légende internationale unifiée pour les cartes archéologiques, dont l'objectif consiste à montrer les corrélations existant entre les différents gisements, et à faire ainsi ressortir "la marche de certaines civilisations et le choix constant des sites" (Chantre, 1876, 941). Le Congrès reprend cet exposé à son compte et désigne une nouvelle commission internationale "pour discuter ce projet et arrêter une légende définitive" (Mortillet Chantre, 1876, 942). Faute de temps, c'est une sous-commission (Mortillet, Chantre) qui se charge de publier ce travail dans les comptes-rendus du Congrès de Stockholm en tenant compte des discussions qui ont eu lieu et des communications écrites qui lui auront été adressées. Le résultat de cette œuvre collective est présenté et permet qu'à Budapest, en 1876, un système de légendes soit adopté. À Paris, en 1900, à l'instigation de A. Voss, le congrès se penche à nouveau sur la question, avec pour objectif d'uniformiser les initiatives nationales sous l'égide du Congrès. A cet effet, Voss (1902, 196) propose de créer une "Commission permanente qui aurait pour mandat d'examiner son projet et de présenter un rapport à la prochaine session". Après de brefs débats sur l'utilité de telles cartes, par nature réductrices d'une réalité complexe, la proposition est renvoyée à l'examen du conseil, lequel décide de créer une commission internationale pour une "entente internationale pour la création d'une légende unique des cartes palethnologiques". En 1906, la cartographie devient une préoccupation importante au congrès de Monaco, puisque sont présentés un rapport de Chantre au nom de la commission créée en 1900, ainsi qu'une communication (Lissauer, 1906). Cependant, l'ensemble s'enlise dans le formalisme et les détails – pour un résultat nul, puisque le choix est fait de se conformer à la légende adoptée autrefois à Budapest.

---
[1] La Société préhistorique française n'a été créée qu'en 1904.

Or, toutes ces discussions autour d'une uniformisation de la cartographie n'intègrent à aucun moment la question en termes patrimoniaux – ne serait-ce qu'à des fins conservatoires, en conférant aux cartes une espèce de rôle de "mémoire" des sites et des monuments.

CONSCIENCE ET MESURES EN FAVEUR DE LA PROTECTION DU PATRIMOINE

La protection repose sur un sentiment (l'intérêt de préserver un patrimoine, pour le présent et l'avenir, d'éventuelles déprédations ou de trop grandes visées mercantiles), une considération objective (la science future pourrait permettre d'en tirer des informations nouvelles qu'il convient de ne pas obérer) et sur des moyens, en particulier juridiques, pour garantir l'ensemble (la mise en place d'un arsenal législatif et réglementaire propre à protéger sites, gisements et pièces). Avec une telle perspective, la réglementation devient un indice objectif du niveau de prise de conscience individuelle et collective.

Pour mettre un terme aux razzias opérées sur leurs antiquités ou pour nourrir le sentiment national en puisant dans leurs racines archéologiques, de nombreux pays européens ont très tôt intégré cette nécessité dans leurs politiques publiques et ont su élaborer des mesures d'inventaire et de protection. Au début du XXe siècle, ce choix fait ainsi ressortir le retard pris par la France en la matière.

Du côté de l'archéologie classique, en Italie, c'est au tout début du XIXe siècle que les premières mesures de protection légale des antiquités et des fouilles ont été prises, mais c'est dans les États pontificaux que la législation a pris naissance dès le *Quattrocento,* avec les humanistes et les artistes "qui ont constitué l'Antiquité en objet historique et l'art en discipline autonome [et qui] étaient corrélativement conduits à valoriser et à protéger les restes antiques" (Riegl, 1984, 12). Ces principes s'affirment avec le temps, essentiellement dans le sens de l'interdiction de la vente des œuvres à l'étranger. Pour les périodes préhistorique et protohistorique, le Danemark est à bien des égards précurseur au plan de la protection du patrimoine archéologique. Les premières mesures de conservation de monuments runiques datent du XVIIe siècle. En 1807, la Commission royale pour la conserva-tion des antiquités est créée, à charge pour elle de veiller sur la conservation des monuments du royaume. Une vaste enquête est lancée à travers le royaume et, sur cette base, le ministère de la justice place, au cours des années 1809-1810, de nombreux monuments de l'antiquité et du Moyen Âge sous la protection de l'État. En 1848, le gouvernement danois ordonne que "tous les assemblages de pierres, tertres funéraires, pierres runiques, fortifications anciennes et ruines de châteaux existant dans les domaines royaux et les bois de l'État [soient] déclarés domaines royaux" (Marsy, 1878, 577), avec maintien de ce statut-même en cas d'aliénation. En 1874, une loi déclenche un vaste mouvement d'inventaire des monu-ments historiques du Danemark, qui sera confié à des archéologues et à des dessinateurs, dont la tâche consiste à décrire les monuments, mais également à désigner ceux qui mériteraient d'être placés sous la protection de la loi. Parallèlement, des fonds sont versés à des propriétaires privés afin de les aider à restaurer certains édifices. À partir de 1815, sous l'influence déterminante de C.J. Thomsen, la Commission royale pour la conservation des antiquités adossée au Musée royal des antiquités va procéder à de nombreuses acquisitions de collections privées, à des fouilles et, surtout, va recueillir des milliers de dons privés.

La France connaît une situation tout à fait différente car le mouvement de protection du patrimoine met beaucoup de temps avant de s'engager. Pourtant, l'État centralisateur français, contrairement au dispositif constitutionnel du fédéralisme suisse (Kaeser, 2004), aurait pu jouer un rôle moteur en la matière. Au sortir des destructions de la Révolution puis tout au long du XIXe siècle, les érudits locaux développent la notion de patrimoine national et le sentiment qu'il est nécessaire de préserver les "monu-ments historiques". Lorsque l'État à son tour se préoccupe de la question, la France ne fait alors que tenter de rattraper son retard, ce que consacre la loi du 30 mars 1887 sur "la conservation des monuments d'art ayant un intérêt historique et artistique".

Au seuil du XXe siècle, l'archéologie préhistorique métropolitaine offre l'apparence d'avoir acquis un début de reconnaissance institutionnelle. La France se dote de normes réglementaires et législatives, mais aussi de structures administratives consultatives, qui intègrent les temps préhistoriques dans leur champ d'application. La Sous-commission des monuments mégalithiques de la Commission des monuments historiques déploie ses activités et le Musée des antiquités nationales, fondé en 1862, demeure la référence obligée des préhistoriens et, malgré le peu de moyens dont il dispose, représente la solution pérenne pour les collections. Les administrations publiques elles-mêmes recommandent à leurs agents de faire preuve de vigilance et d'éviter les destructions intempestives. Mais cet ensemble ne peut masquer une réalité: la préhistoire demeure une aventure essentielle-ment individuelle, dont le lettré naturaliste de province est l'archétype; aucun cadre juridique réellement contraig-nant ne vient organiser les recherches et canaliser des ardeurs parfois dévastatrices. Dans le contexte de quête de "l'objet pour l'objet" (favorisé par la primauté de l'approche typologique qui donne un sens et une position chronologique à la pièce), alors au cœur de la démarche des préhistoriens, le processus de régulation, qui s'est enclenché à partir de la mise en œuvre des premières mesures de protection du patrimoine, ne présente pour seuls avantages que de leur permettre de travailler en paix tout en leur offrant des garanties de propriétaire sur les gisements qu'ils exploitent.

Objets de collection, de commerce et de convoitise, les pièces préhistoriques se voient reconnaître une valeur moindre que n'importe quel autre document patrimonial. Sans doute souffrent-elles de la hiérarchie entre les "deux pôles de la curiosité antiquaire", c'est-à-dire entre les "antiquités ethniques" et les antiquités classiques, ces dernières étant porteuses d'une valeur universelle de beau et de vrai (Pomian, 2003, 176-191). "Un objet se voit attribuer une valeur, lorsqu'il est protégé, conservé ou reproduit", c'est-à-dire qu'il doit pour ce faire être "chargé de signification", ce qui lui confère sa valeur dès lors qu'il n'est pas "utile" (Pomian, 1987, 43) Les pièces préhistoriques n'ont comme légitimité que celle accordée aux témoins, aux indices matériels d'un passé lointain difficile à recomposer. Jusqu'à la première guerre mondiale, même recueillies *in situ*, elles ne tirent leur valeur réelle qu'indépendamment du contexte et de toute corrélation stratigraphique. Celle-ci repose sur l'attention que le fouilleur voudra bien leur porter sur le moment, sur l'intérêt scientifique qu'il leur accordera (marqueur chronologique, "fossile directeur") et sur les soins que le collectionneur apportera à leur conservation. Force est de constater que les congrès IAAP ne se préoccupent pas de ces questions.

LA QUESTION DE LA REGLEMENTATION DANS LES CONGRES IAAP: UNE AFFAIRE ESSENTIELLEMENT FRANCO-FRANÇAISE

Les sessions CIAPP offrent aux préhistoriens français l'occasion de se confronter aux pratiques contemporaines dans les autres pays. De retour des sessions de Copenhague (1869) et de Stockholm (1874), tous célèbrent ces populations scandinaves conscientisées et le dynamisme des États nordiques engagés dans une espèce d'introspection patriotique à travers la célébration du patrimoine archéologique: "Le patriotisme des Danois, servi par une énergie à la fois active et patiente, se retrouve partout. Il a été pour une bonne part dans la formation de leurs plus beaux musées; il assure le développement futur de ceux qui laissent encore à désirer." (Quatrefages, 1870, 967) Mais, chose étonnante, aucun ne tire de leçon pour son propre pays de cet enthousiasme en faveur des antiquités. Au contraire, les sessions CIAAP qui se tiennent à Paris sont le prétexte de débats essentiellement franco-français sur la question des fouilles, certainement en raison du défaut d'instance nationale dans laquelle aborder et résoudre ces difficultés.

Lors de la session de 1889, une vive discussion s'engage après une intervention de l'anthropologue Paul Topinard, qui s'insurgeait contre le peu de considération accordée aux restes humains dans les fouilles. Selon lui, le fouilleur (non le gisement) est le "trait d'union" entre les deux spécialités scientifiques du Congrès (paléo-anthropologie et paléo-ethnographie). Or "pour un naturaliste ou un archéologue préparé il y a cent fouilleurs que je qualifierais volontiers d'amateurs, ayant les connaissances les plus opposées, pratiquant des fouilles en manière de distraction et conduisant de front leurs occupations ordinaires" (Topinard, 1891, 382). Le manque de formation des fouilleurs expliquerait grandement le peu d'attention qu'ils accordent aux restes humains par rapport aux objets et "une station touchée est une station détruite", perdue pour les générations futures (*Ibid.*, 390). Comme la question des origines de l'homme est par essence internationale, puisque "l'idée de race est absolument étrangère à l'idée de nationalité" (*Ibid.*, 391), Topinard souhaite que le CIAAP nomme une commission afin de rédiger des instructions pour les fouilleurs "dans lesquelles on attirerait leur attention sur la nécessité: 1° de procéder méthodiquement dans les fouilles de façon à avoir la date exacte des objets et ossements; 2° de porter une attention égale à la récolte et à la conservation des crânes et des objets archéologiques." (*Ibid.*, 391-392). Heinrich Schliemann soutient la démarche, tout comme Émile Cartailhac, qui souligne que les fouilleurs "se moquent absolument des débris humains et ne tiennent qu'aux objets". D'autres, comme Georges Vacher de Lapouge, préféreraient que les pouvoirs publics prennent conscience de la nécessité de préserver ces restes. Certains, comme Adrien et Gabriel de Mortillet, prennent en revanche la défense des amateurs contre ce qu'ils estiment être une injuste sévérité. Les débats ne permettant pas de trouver une position commune, la décision est renvoyée au conseil du Congrès, qui décide de créer la commission (dont la composition est exclusivement française) – à charge pour elle de déposer ses conclusions à l'ouverture de la prochaine session. Ainsi, à défaut de doctrine internationale, se trouve confortée l'approche traditionnelle française, qui consiste à ne pas s'immiscer dans le travail des préhistoriens et d'exclure tout esprit de contrainte.

Si en 1889, la discussion reste sans suite (dans la mesure où aucun rapport n'est présenté à Moscou en 1892), en revanche, en 1900, le débat porte sur l'encadrement voire explicitement les restrictions à apporter aux pratiques de terrain. À Paris, Auguste Cancalon présente une pétition de la Société positiviste afin de "provoquer des mesures de protection pour la conservation des stations de l'époque quaternaire". Il souhaite que le CIAAP émette lui aussi un tel vœu (Cancalon, 1902, 192): "La postérité s'étonnera, à bon droit, de l'insuffisante protection qui [...] est accordée [aux monuments de l'époque paléolithique], lorsque d'autres monuments, moins intéressants et moins significatifs, sont classés comme monuments publics." Son souci va même au-delà puisqu'il s'agit de favoriser la création de musées de site et de mener un vaste mouvement d'éducation populaire en demandant "que des notions, au moins sommaires sur la préhistoire, soient introduites dans les programmes de l'enseignement secondaire et même primaire." (*Ibid.*) La discussion s'engage entre les participants à la session et évolue vers une question plus fondamentale: la préservation des gisements et donc la valeur des fouilles qui y sont menées tant du point de vue de la méthode que du professionnalisme des chercheurs. En d'autres termes: ne conviendrait-il pas de restreindre la liberté de fouilles?

Salomon Reinach déclare sans détour qu'"Il faudrait interdire aux personnes non qualifiées de fouiller des gisements qu'ils ne peuvent que ravager au lieu de les explorer scientifiquement." (*Ibid.*) Il s'agit là d'un argument contre lequel Adrien de Mortillet s'inscrit en faux. Partisan d'une approche libérale, il mise sur l'émulation entre les fouilleurs pour favoriser le dynamisme scientifique et "réclame pour les fouilleurs liberté pleine et entière" (Cancalon, 1902, 193). Or, l'introduction d'une réglementation spécifique aux opérations de fouille ou la définition d'un niveau d'exigence quelconque auront des conséquences directes sur le statut individuel du fouilleur, avec le risque de brider l'autonomie des préhistoriens amateurs.

Rompent avec cette philosophie ancienne, des savants comme Marcellin Boule qui clame depuis des années que "pour faire de bonnes fouilles il est nécessaire d'avoir des compétences toutes spéciales" (*Ibid.*), mais également Cartailhac, Gustave Chauvet et Léonce Manouvrier. La position de ce dernier n'est pas étonnante: cela fait près de vingt ans qu'il tente d'attirer l'attention des anthropologues, et en particulier celle des membres de la Société d'anthropologie de Paris, sur la nécessité de protéger les gisements préhistoriques, de les mettre à l'abri du vandalisme des collectionneurs. Quant au recours à la loi, Manouvrier s'interroge sur son opportunité et se positionne à mi-chemin entre une liberté totale et une réglementation générale: "Peut-être mettrait-elle simplement le sort des stations néolithiques ou paléolithiques à la merci d'autorités administratives peu compétentes ou bien trop disposées à tenir compte de considérations extra-scientifiques. Il faudrait que la loi se bornât à une prohibition visant toute personne non formellement accréditée pour une fouille déterminée. La compétence des explorateurs devrait être attestée par une société anthropologique." (Cancalon, 1902, 193-194) Dans l'immédiat, un appel à l'opinion publique, afin de l'instruire des dégâts constatés et "des exigences que comporte une étude vraiment scientifique des documents de notre préhistoire" (*Ibid.*, 194), permettrait selon lui d'éviter bien des destructions. Pour ce faire, le CIAAP peut jouer un rôle déterminant en prenant position et en profitant du relais de la presse.

Sur la suggestion du Secrétaire général Verneau, le vœu proposé par Cancalon est renvoyé à l'examen du conseil permanent du Congrès. Là, John Evans estime que la discussion devrait être ajournée dans la mesure où elle ne lui semble pas relever des compétences du CIAAP, voire être en contradiction avec les législations de certains pays. Il s'interroge même de savoir si le problème n'est pas strictement français, auquel cas il pense que l'Académie des Inscriptions et belles-lettres serait qualifiée pour intervenir. Après des discussions, le texte est adopté, mais sous une forme différente de la version originale. Il met en exergue le recours aux pouvoirs publics et au législateur pour que les monuments soient protégés et que la licence des fouilles soit restreinte: "1° Que les pouvoirs publics assurent, par une loi, la conservation d'un certain nombre de cavernes habitées par l'homme préhistorique. 2° Que, sans porter atteinte au droit de propriété, ils s'inspirent de l'exemple donné il y a deux siècles en Suède pour interdire les fouilles archéologiques dans les cavernes, restes d'habitations et tombeaux, aux personnes qui ne seraient pas munies, à cet effet, d'un permis de l'administration compétente, laquelle pourrait toujours revendiquer la surveillance directe des fouilles et retirer un permis dont il serait fait abus." Cartailhac est invité par le conseil à rédiger un rapport sommaire sur la législation des pays étrangers relativement aux fouilles, rapport destiné à "servir de préambule à une communication éventuelle à la presse des vœux qui viennent d'être adoptés." (*Congrès*, 1902, 24).

À l'issue de ces discussions, le secrétaire général du congrès rend compte, lors de la sixième séance plénière, des décisions prises par le conseil puisque celles-ci doivent être ratifiées par le Congrès pour être adoptées. Une nouvelle fois les débats s'ouvrent et Mortillet et Émile Collin "protestent contre le vœu ayant pour objet d'interdire les fouilles aux personnes qui ne seraient pas munies d'un permis de l'administration compétente et réclament la liberté absolue des recherches pour tous les fouilleurs." Mise aux voix, la proposition du conseil est néanmoins adoptée par 27 suffrages pour et 19 contre. Dans la foulée, la double demande est adressée au ministre de l'Instruction publique du gouvernement français.

Cet épisode montre très clairement la ligne de fracture qui existe alors chez les préhistoriens en France, entre la prépondérance de la défense formelle des droits individuels des chercheurs et une vision collective et patrimoniale. Ces divisions trahissent des clivages sociaux et structurels qui dépassent le domaine strict de la science, l'opposition, en somme, entre deux mondes: entre Paris et la province, les institutions centralisées d'État et les sociétés savantes provinciales, entre les professionnels (hommes de laboratoires et d'institutions, universitaires, conservateurs) et les amateurs (érudits qui font vivre l'archéologie de terrain). À l'évidence, les discussions de cette session CIAAP ne sont pas à dimension internationale. Ses participants ont fait le deuil d'une doctrine transnationale de préservation du patrimoine. Les Français favorables à une action instrumentalisent le Congrès pour faire pression sur les pouvoirs publics nationaux qui se désintéressent de l'archéologie préhistorique. En pure perte, en définitive, puisque le ministre de l'Instruction publique leur adressera une réponse en forme de fin de non-recevoir. Quoi qu'il en soit, les positions des uns et des autres sont devenues publiques et ce premier affrontement n'est que le premier d'une longue série qui ne trouvera sa conclusion qu'en 1941 avec la loi Carcopino imposée par le régime de Vichy (et toujours en vigueur actuellement) (Hurel, 2004, 38-344).

CONCLUSION

Les sessions des CIAAP n'ont pas permis de faire émerger une conscience patrimoniale internationale. À l'image des autres congrès, les CIAAP ont conscience de leur peu d'efficacité à faire appliquer leurs vœux et résolutions (Rasmussen, 1995, 143). Mais, sur cette matière, la volonté de faire émerger une expression commune, la "construction d'un consensus" (*Ibid.*, 145), n'existe même pas. Le Congrès ne concède qu'une position marginale à toutes les questions patrimoniales. Cette dimension, au cœur pourtant de la démarche du préhistorien (que ce soit en tant que fouilleur ou collectionneur), demeure contingente et exclue du champ scientifique et, paradoxalement, de sessions où s'élabore un idéal de Préhistoire indivise. Pourtant, ce sujet était *a priori* suffisamment transversal et fédérateur dans ses multiples dimensions (méthodes de fouilles, gestion – y compris en termes réglementaires – des gisements exploités, protection des sites, devenir des pièces mises au jour) pour être porteur du mythe identitaire et trouver sa place dans les débats. Or, à aucun moment, il n'intègre le champ international, comme nous avons pu le voir avec la question de la cartographie, ou est noyé dans des considérations à visées strictement nationales (Paris 1889 et 1900) et renvoyé comme tel à la compétence interne des nations.

Au-delà de cet échec, cette attitude nous permet de dégager plusieurs enseignements. Il s'agit tout d'abord d'une caractérologie de la communauté des préhistoriens marquée par la nature essentiellement individualiste de leur démarche scientifique. Ensuite, le déni de toute valeur propre, autre que scientifique, aux objets. En effet, la position accordée aux pièces illustre la place marginale reconnue à l'interaction gisement/objets et par conséquent le caractère longtemps accessoire des méthodes de fouille. Cette archéologie *hic et nunc* frappe par l'absence de projection dans l'avenir. Élément important au point de se demander si, au tournant du XXe siècle, ne domine pas le sentiment que l'essentiel des découvertes est déjà accompli. Reconnaître le patrimoine c'est envisager un avenir scientifique différent du présent, prendre conscience de droits scientifiques à venir et donc à préserver. Or, pendant toute la période ici étudiée, cette représentation de l'archéologie fait défaut.

Bibliographie

BERR, H. (1908) – Sur l'organisation des congrès internationaux. *Revue de synthèse historique*. Paris. 16: 2, p. 216-217.

CANCALON (1902) – "La conservation des stations quaternaires". In *Congrès international d'anthropologie et d'archéologie préhistoriques. Compte-rendu de la 12e session. Paris 1900*. Paris: Masson.

CHANTRE, E. (1876) – La légende internationale pour les cartes préhistoriques. In *Congrès international d'archéologie et d'anthropologie préhistoriques, Compte-rendu de la 7e session, Stockholm, 1874*. Stockholm: Imprimerie centrale, p. 937-942.

CONGRES international d'archéologie et d'anthropologie préhistoriques, Compte-rendu de la 2e session, Paris, 1868. Paris: C. Reinwald.

CONGRES international d'anthropologie et d'archéologie préhistoriques. Compte-rendu de la 12e session. Paris 1900. Paris: Masson, 1902.

HUBERT, H. (1900) – Congrès d'anthropologie et d'archéologie préhistoriques. *Revue de synthèse historique*. Paris. 1: 2, p. 219-228.

HUREL, A. (2004) – *L'institutionnalisation de l'archéologie préhistorique en France métropolitaine (1852-1941) et l'Institut de paléontologie humaine*. Thèse de doctorat. Université Paris 4 Sorbonne. 661 p.

KAESER, M.-A. (2004) – Les prémices d'une politique archéologique au XIXe siècle. *Revue historique neuchâteloise*. 1-2: p. 15-32.

LARTET, É. (1868) – Discours de clôture. In *Congrès international d'archéologie et d'anthropologie préhistoriques, Compte-rendu de la 2e session. Paris, 1867*. Paris: C. Reinwald, p. 425-426.

LISSAUER, A. (1906) – Sur l'origine et l'importance des cartes de types préhistoriques. In *Congrès international d'archéologie et d'anthropologie préhistoriques, Compte-rendu de la 13e session, Monaco, 1906*. Monaco: Imprimerie de Monaco, vol. 2, p. 163-166.

MARSY, DE. (1878) – De la législation danoise sur la conservation des monuments historiques et des antiquités nationales. *Bulletin monumental*. 6: p. 572-584.

MORTILLET, G. de; CHANTRE, E. (1876) – Rapport de la commission nommée au Congrès de Stockholm. In *Congrès international d'archéologie et d'anthropologie préhistoriques, Compte-rendu de la 7e session, Stockholm, 1874*. Stockholm: Imprimerie centrale, p. 942-960.

POMIAN, K. (1987) – *Collectionneurs, amateurs et curieux. Paris, Venise: XVIe-XVIIIe siècle*. Paris: Gallimard. 367 p.

POMIAN, K. (2003) – *Des saintes reliques à l'art moderne. Venise-Chicago XIIIe-XXe siècle*. Paris: Gallimard. 369 p.

QUATREFAGES, A. de. (1870) – Le congrès international d'archéologie préhistorique (session de Copenhague). – I. Les musées antéhistoriques de Copenhague. *Revue des deux mondes*. 86: p. 952-978.

RASMUSSEN, A. (1995) – *L'internationale scientifique (1890-1914)*. Thèse de doctorat. École des hautes études en sciences sociales. 816 p.

RIEGL, A. (1984) – *Le culte moderne des monuments. Son essence et sa genèse*. Paris: Le Seuil. 123 p.

TOPINARD, P. (1891) – La paléo-anthropologie. In *Congrès international d'anthropologie et d'archéologie préhistoriques. Compte-rendu de la 10e session. Paris 1889*. Paris: Ernest Leroux, p. 382-397.

VERNEAU, R. (1902) – Discours du secrétaire général. In *Congrès international d'archéologie et d'anthropologie préhistoriques, Compte-rendu de la 12ᵉ session, Paris, 1900*. Paris: Masson, p. X.

VIRCHOW, R. (1892) – Les changements dans les problèmes du Congrès international d'archéologie et d'anthropologie préhistoriques. In *Congrès international d'archéologie et d'anthropologie préhistoriques, Compte-rendu de la 11ᵉ session, Moscou, 1892*. Moscou: Imprimerie de l'Université impériale, p. 223-228.

VOGT, C. (1868) – *Congrès international d'archéologie et d'anthropologie préhistoriques, Compte-rendu de la 2ᵉ session*, Paris: C. Reinwald. p. 58.

VOSS, A. (1902) – Projet de cartographie préhistorique internationale. In *Congrès international d'anthropologie et d'archéologie préhistoriques. Compte-rendu de la 12ᵉ session. Paris 1900*. Paris: Masson. p. 195-197.

A SCANDINAVIAN VIEW OF THE BEGINNING OF CONGRESS TIMES

Jarl NORDBLADH

Göteborg University, Dpt of Archaeology and Ancient History, Box 200, SE 405 30 Göteborg, Sweden,
J.Nordbladh@archaeology.gu.se

Abstract: Prehistoric Archaeology started its public and professional meetings within the first Conferences in Natural Sciences. Many scholars were eager to meet colleagues in an international context, in order to present their own research, to learn about scientific novelties, and even to observe selected artefacts and go on site excursions. As a parallel phenomenon, there were often other kinds of presentations, such as scientific instruments, visual apparatus and even shows — a mixture of knowledge and entertainment. These congresses were also important social events, which received the visit of royalties anxious to be seen as protectors of and stimuli for the development of society.
The early archaeological congresses certainly learnt from the even earlier ones — those of natural sciences — how to organize, inform about and select boards for specific tasks, as well as to develop protocol regulations such as the choice of languages allowed, the order of speech, etc.
Key Words: Conference – Congress – Disciplinary history – Entertainment – International – Meeting – National – Prehistorian – Scandinavia – Scientist – Student

Résumé: C'est dans le cadre des congrès de naturalistes que l'archéologie préhistorique a connu ses premières réunions publiques et professionnelles. De nombreux savant étaient désireux de rencontrer des collègues dans un contexte international, afin de présenter leurs propres travaux, de s'enquérir de l'actualité de la recherche, d'observer certains matériaux sélectionnés et de s'engager dans des excursions sur le terrain. Parallèlement, ces manifestations accueillaient souvent d'autres types de présentations, telles que des démonstrations d'instruments scientifiques, d'appareillages visuels, et même des spectacles offrant un mélange de divertissement et d'enseignement savant. Ces congrès représentaient également d'importants événements sociaux, qui pouvaient accueillir la visite de membres des familles royales désireux de s'afficher en protecteurs et en promoteurs du développement social.
Les premiers congrès archéologiques ont certainement tiré avantages de ces expériences antérieures – celles des sciences naturelles – quant à l'organisation pratique et scientifique, ainsi que la promotion des manifestations, la mise en place d'une réglementation, le choix des langues officielles, le protocole, etc.
Mots-clé: Conférence – Congrès – Histoire disciplinaire – Divertissement – International – Réunion – National – Préhistorien – Scandinavie – Savants – Etudiants

INTRODUCTION

The history of archaeological congresses could be a rather quick and rational affair; but with such a product, we would probably learn very little. Instead, I'll try to exploit another path, in order to learn how archaeologists and people interested in prehistory and "national antiquities" have encountered each other and how they have communicated their knowledge – over time. In this way, the congresses, national and international, can be considered as a special form of meeting, which was created around the middle of the 19th century, and had other structures and uses than the already existing learned societies and academies (Congrès Internationaux 1960; Kaeser 2006; Sommer & Struwe 2006; Wetherall 1998).

By integrating the congresses into the social web of field archaeology, heritage preservation, museums, universities, academies, societies and printing works, it is also possible to relate it with the respective political and economic situations, as well as the ways communication could take, from a technological point of view.

This historiographic enterprise is highly dependent on the state of archival documentation: the documents selected determine the outcome of the study. Comprehensive, well structured archives will be strong co-workers, while dispersed, badly kept documents will be more silent. Our task is also to evaluate the quality of the documents, their once exercised powers, and how to deal with such information, which can be diverging, according to different documents. Planning documents for the congresses, their programmes and publications, but also letters, diaries, reports in newspapers and scientific journals are source materials of vital importance. After some time, also pictures and photographs have to be analyzed regarding time, place, and persons present.

FROM LEARNED PERSON TO SCIENTIST

Congresses did not just appear at a certain time. It is possible to identify several attempts to create organizations for intellectual cooperation on an international level. Most of them ended up as utopian plans for a "Republic of Letters". Already in the 17th century, it seems that these plans were reflections on the hard effects of extensive wars — a try to change the conditions of intellectual work and life (Sörlin 1994). Bengt Skytte, for example, a Swedish diplomat and linguist, being also the Vice-Chancellor of Dorpat University, suggested to several authorities such as Charles II, Friedrich Wilhelm of Brandenburg, and Colbert, in the middle of the 17th century, the creation of a centre of learning, an Academy for the People, with research and education in all fields of science and arts, which had to include a library, a laboratory, a botanical garden, a museum and a printing press. With full academic freedom, all religions and all nationalities were to be allowed in this Academy, which could offer a refuge in case of war.

Through these utopian plans it can be seen that learned persons were reflecting on the conditions of their work – but also that there was a new appreciation of what a scientist could or should be – a new social category, not aiming at a profession – in our terms. He, as it is only men we talk about here, had to be well educated, using his knowledge both in administration as a bureaucrat, and in his studies as an independent intellectual. Nowadays, it is not so easy to understand how such a division could be kept in reality. It is probably a wish from some learned persons not to be integrated in state affairs, which also suggests that they saw it as a threatening possibility. The scientific world before the 19th century was perceived as a whole corpus, with no clear divisions: a single person could survey it all, guided by the search for Truth.

I mentioned that the learned society was a male one. Some women scientists could be members of academies (mostly because of their noble background), but rules for membership did not mention female members: an intellectual collaboration between the sexes was an impossible thought. There are even examples showing that the rules were changed later, in order to explicitly prohibit female entrance. On the other hand, the presence of women is rather unclear, as they may have accompanied their husbands, fathers and brothers on certain occasions, which are hardly mentioned in the documents.

Later on, in the 1830s, female rebellion occured, as women suddenly and uninvited, attended meetings of the BAAS (The British Association for the Advancement of Science), even representing the majority of the assembly (Eriksson 1991, p. 236-7). What a chock for many men, but also an inspiration for changes towards democracy!

The learned person should strive to be a prototype, a gentleman of excellent character and moral, a product of free studies and free, self-chosen contents. You can see that the ideas from the Enlightenment were still current.

This "learned person" type was later to be replaced by another kind of individuality – the scientist – who had different relations to the research field. These scientists were more concentrated on data collection in relation to interpretation and abstract theories, and more specialized on a certain subjects or material categories. Furthermore, many of them were radical in political terms – striving for the enforcement of democratic principles, for the union of small states to greater Nations, such as in Germany and Italy, and for social changes within societies. This does not mean however, that they, by necessity, were radical in their scientific work.

NATIONAL – INTERNATIONAL

The effects of the Napoleonic wars were striking – of course it was a defeat and a collapse of many visions of a necessary new society. A promise became a failure. New concepts of nation and territory diverged. It became even more important to reinvent a secure national identity, based on people, language, land, and history (Det nya Norden efter Napoleon 2004).

For the sake of the Nordic Countries, Finland became part of the Russian Empire, parts of Northen Germany left Sweden, Denmark lost Norway (but not Island) and Norway was forced into a not wanted union with Sweden. Later, Denmark lost most of its southern districts to German Countries. So – and this is important – the time of a strong development of prehistoric research in Scandinavia coincided with considerable political changes, mostly of a painful character. Three of the once five Swedish universities were now lost: Dorpat in Estonia (earlier), Åbo in Finland, and Greifswald in Northern Germany.

With this background situation there had to be a hidden agenda behind the evolving archaeological missions, which followed two main features: the organisation of materials within museums, and the care of ancient monuments in the landscape. A certain competition can be observed between a rather limited group of prehistorians; obviously, the early congresses allowed to extend this competition into an international forum, where the competitors could search for support and recognition.

Nations were eager to use the scientists and their scientific work for state reasons: science became part of the national production, both in real terms and in ideological terms. In this perspective, scientists found themselves in a difficult situation. They were claiming for national progress, and developing schemata for the national politics of research one the one hand. And on the other hand, they strived to show the nations and also the individuals' will to co-operate. Practically, this lead the scientists to express doubts and diverging opinions – without insulting the organisers of the respective congresses and their host countries.

ENTERTAINMENT

In the beginning of the 19th century congresses were part of a new way to meet and to show, to trade and to make decisions, such as industrial fairs, world fairs containing almost every aspect of human knowledge and parallel to all this, a side of entertainment – which made use of technical skills and illusions (Mûller-Scheessel 2001). The cities were illuminated and galleries remained open in the evenings. The day was prolonged and the evening became an exciting addition, a twilight zone, for amusing activities.

From the personal diaries we can learn about the public success of dioramas with natural or historical themes, as well as air balloon demonstrations (Altick 1978; Eriksson 1959). The rich possibilities to meet a new technical world also integrated with the very way of travelling, by steamboat with timetables using both open sea and canals, railways, and resting places such as hotels with sometimes more than a hundred of rooms, and collective, anonymous eating at restaurants. Also telegraphs and fast mail with standardized costs and stamps made communication easier.

From the point of view of disciplinary history it is interesting to observe the way researchers have limited their subjects, often omitting the working conditions of the scientists and their daily life and experiences. Just to give an example: it is quite possible that a general interest in history and prehistory is derived from contacts with panoramas and dioramas, and other kinds of arrangements with models, wax cabinets and different illusory tricks as a first and strong and surprising experience. Museum displays may very well be an archaeological illusion in itself, a wish-for situation developed by the archaeologists themselves, which were able to produce an attractive, persuasive and educating historical product. Such effects probably still last up today, with the visions produced by digital restitutions.

BERLIN 1828

Let us now turn to a concrete setting, which appears very important, considering its influence in the creation of other congresses, in England, France, Italy, or Scandinavia.

In terms of academic development, the Berlin University, created as late as 1810, became a prototype for a new generation, being foremost educated in general and within cultural frames. There were about forty universities in the German Countries around 1800, while England had two and Scandinavia five, with very varying programmes but also stimulating relations. The Berlin mission was to create a social and cultural elite on qualifications of education. A harmonic, moral, cultural man was the intended end result — not a profession. However, knowledge had also to be based on scientific methods and criticism, careful observation and specific control of proofs and evidence. The Berlin University also demonstrated the Prussian resistance against Napoleonic occupation.

Berlin became a city of the world and attracted different activities. One of these was the first Meeting for German Researchers in Natural Sciences and for Medical Doctors. The meetings were German speaking and organized every year. The seventh meeting, again in Berlin, in 1828, became outstanding also because many delegates came from foreign countries (Eriksson 1959; Eriksson 1991, p. 19-54).

For the first time you could see a collective concern from the students, now forming part of society as a special group with special demands and obligations. Student meetings were hold, for example in Jena in 1818, with participants from all German States. Student leaders appeared and talked openly in society. The students also burnt what they thought to be bad books, of low quality or politically not acceptable.

The authorities worried much about the situation. Meetings were prohibited, censorships were executed. The arguments for a national unification of Germany were seen as dangerous for the states. Freedom of speech and for the press was not seen as being of general interest – on the contrary. In other words, the political situation, when the first congresses started, was far from stable and inviting.

The Berlin meeting of 1828 was not organized and labelled as an international one. However, it was visited by many scholars from abroad; some of them were highly interested in the structure of the meeting and how it was carried out. Lorenz Oken and Alexander von Humboldt were the leading figures, attracting colleagues from many other European countries. Charles Babbage, for instance, was there, as well as the French antiquarian Arcisse de Caumont. The Swedish delegation was limited, but especially Sven Nilsson was impressed, being on his first tour out of Scandinavia.

Babbage got inspiration in Berlin to create the British Association for the Advancement of Science (BAAS) in 1831. Caumont was of another character, being totally against the concentration in France of all institutes in Paris, and he formed several scientific organizations shortly afterwards, such as the Congrès Scientifique de France in 1833, the Congrès archéologique in 1834, and the Institut des Provinces in 1839 (Eriksson 1991, p.55-83, 100-102).

The Berlin meeting was a striking manifestation of bourgeois sociability. It was rather unpredictable, new, exciting, but also politically provocative. However, it managed to attract both royalties and members of the government. Even special music was composed for the occasion, by Friedrich Mendelssohn!

SCANDINAVIA

Turning to Scandinavia, now, the visit in Berlin actually meant a lot for the Swedish participants. However, this was not to remain the only Scandinavian visit: in 1830, as many as 79 Scandinavians attended the meeting, this time in Hamburg (Eriksson 1991, p. 154). Soon, there was a suggestion to create a new organization of its own, uniting persons involved in the natural sciences. These were seen as a collective, including disciplines such as geology, zoology, biology, medicine, but also physics and chemistry. Prehistoric themes were welcomed, as they touched upon many of the existing disciplines. It is quite possible that the Scandinavians with interest in prehistory and archaeology consciously chose to be part of these meetings, in a process of searching for an identity, which should not be the classical one, that of learned scholars. The term "scientist", created at the time of the first meeting in BAAS in 1831, could hopefully give this specific position – with a stress on working within clear, systematic methods, and trying to prove their case with the help of excavated materials.

The first Scandinavian meeting for natural scientists was took place in 1839, in Göteborg, Sweden, with 93 participants (Eriksson 1991). Sven Nilsson was very active in the creation. There were troubles to make it real both locally and on national levels. Also, there were worries about the quantitative participation. But it turned out well; the meetings went on (but not on a yearly basis) on varying places, in 1840, 1842, 1844, 1847, 1851, 1856, 1860, 1863, etc. Both Sven Nilsson, J.J.A. Worsaae and later Oscar Montelius used these occasions to present or defend their ideas.

The meetings were influenced by the new Scandinavian vision of a common past and a solidarity, a sort of revival of the united Nordic kingdom of the medieval queen Margarete I. Of course, these thoughts were seen as a threat to the Swedish and Danish courts; politically, the official relations between these countries were under restrictions. Swedish officials were not allowed to stay several days in Denmark without special permission, and Danish historians travelling in Sweden worked also as agents of the state, trying to get political information from members of the government. Even Christian Jürgensen Thomsen had been considered as a potential spy, during his 1820 travel in Skåne (southern Sweden).

Under those circumstances, the Scandinavian meetings meant a lot in recreating the Swedish-Danish (read Lund-Copenhagen) relations for the scientists. Copenhagen was very damaged by the English fleet in 1807, the most intensive cannonade before the Second World War, and the economic situation was very bad. The self-understanding was in trouble. However the liberal politics were mostly nation-bound. At the meeting in Christiania (later Oslo), in 1844, there were worries about the possible participation of persons of Jewish origin: Jews were not allowed in Norway. However, no incident happened.

A great deal of the historical discussions circled around the relations between prehistoric finds and the territories of the contemporary nation states. Pure political arguments laid behind claims about which country being the oldest one. Iceland was of particular concern, seen either as a common Nordic area, or as the result of Norwegian expansion only.

New political agents and ideas were introduced, for which history became an important argument. In the 1860s, Swedish museums we beginning to be formed, both nationally and regionally. There was also an attempt to create an all-Nordic museum in Stockholm, but this creation was never realized – being too grandiose; the museum became exclusively ethnological, but it kept its name, though.

In 1870, the Swedish Society for Ancient Monuments (Svenska Fornminnesföreningen) was formed, mainly as a protest against the established, Central Board of Antiquities (Riksantikvarieämbetet). This testifies to a conflict of interests, a clash between the professional archaeology and the devoted amateurs: the access to the finds and the "confiscation" of remarkable objects in the periphery to be included in the National Historical Museum, in the capital of Stockholm.

Organizing scientific congresses became part of the national programme and a symbol of progression and power. Denmark hosted its first international archaeological conference in 1869, followed by Sweden five years later. The conferences had now grown so much, that they almost died out – from overwork.

CONCLUSIONS

The early congresses, national and international, were created as a combination of political aims, scientific pride, and a will and longing for direct, personal, face-to-face contacts within the scientific society. Unity was searched for, but was hard to obtain.

Personal relations were vital for the continuation of the wandering congresses; they became important also for the development of the discipline.

More comprehensive archaeological problems were preferred to local problems, such as chronologies, geographies, densities. Phenomena which were recognized over the national borders could for example show that the vision of a Scandinavian co-existence could be grounded on historical arguments.

There was a competition about the recognition of the oldest Nordic country. Norway also claimed to be the origin for Iceland. Such claims obviously threatened the idea of a common Scandinavian co-existence.

Museums were presenting new arrangements and excavations were carried out – mostly for the honour of the congresses.

Parallel to the scientific part of the congresses, other arrangements were taken, mainly with entertainment purposes – night life, for instance, which expressed a bourgeois life style in cosmopolitan cities. Many inventions were introduced in such circumstances.

The early congresses with partly archaeological contents had little to do with universities, where archaeological chairs and departments most often were missing.

While the more downright international archaeological congresses started in 1865, a structure and a know-how of their carrying out was already at hand, from earlier activities.

Finally, it is interesting to reflect on that the societal and technical development, mainly construction work, which brought up so many new prehistoric finds and monuments, through coal mining, canals, railways, harbours and city planning, was the same development which made easy travelling to, from and within congresses possible. There is also a moment of speed introduced, a new dimension of communication, in transport, in the spread of scientific ideas, as well as in the circulation of fresh information, called "news".

Acknowledgements

The research on which this article is based was undertaken at Göteborg University, Department of archaeology, in the framework of the AREA network, with the support of the Culture 2000 programme of the European Commission.

References

ALTICK, R. (1978) – The shows of London: a panoramic history of exhibitions, 1600-1862. Cambridge, Belkamp Press of Harvard University Press.

LES CONGRÈS INTERNATIONAUX de 1681 à 1899 (1960) – Liste Complète. Publication UAI No 164, Documents No 8. Union des Associations Internationales. Bruxelles, Palais d'Egmont.

ERIKSSON, G. (1959) – "Till Wetenskapernas Ära". Svenska intryck från naturforskarmötet i Berlin 1828. *Lychnos. Lärdomshistoriska Samfundets Årsbok*, p. 88-129.

ERIKSSON, N. (1991) – "I Andans Kraft, på Sannings Stråt...". De skandinaviska naturforskarmötena 1839 – 1936. Acta Universitatis Gothoburgensis. Gothenburg Studies in the History of Science and Ideas; 12. Göteborg.

KAESER, M-A. (2006) – The First Establishment of Prehistoric Science: The Shortcomings of Autonomy. *Die Anfänge der ur- und frühgeschichtlichen Archäologie als akademisches Fach (1890-1930) im europäischen Vergleich. Internationale Tagung an der Humboldt-Universität zu Berlin vom 13.-16. März 2003*. Johan Callmer, Michael Meyer, Ruth Struwe und Claudia Theune eds. Rahden, Verlag Marie Leidorf, p. 149-160.

DET NYA NORDEN EFTER NAPOLEON (2004) – *25:e Nordiska historikermötet. Stockholm den 4-8 augusti 2004*. Max Engman & Åke Sandström eds. Acta Universitatis Stockholmiensis. Stockholm Studies in History; 73. Stockholm, Almqvist & Wiksell International.

MÜLLER-SCHEESSEL, N. (2001) – Fair Prehistory: archaeological exhibits at French *Expositions Universelles. Antiquity* 75, p. 391-401.

SOMMER, U. & STRUWE, R. (2006) – Bemerkungen zur prähistorischen Archäologie an deutschen Universitäten im 19. Jahrhundert. *Die Anfänge der ur- und frühgeschichtlichen Archäologie als akademisches Fach (1890-1930) im europäischen Vergleich. Internationale Tagung an der Humboldt-Universität zu Berlin vom 13.-16. März 2003*. Johan Callmer, Michael Meyer, Ruth Struwe und Claudia Theune eds. Rahden, Verlag Marie Leidorf, p. 23-42.

SÖRLIN, S. (1994) – *De lärdas republic: om vetenskapens internationella tendenser*. Malmö, Liber-Hermod i samarbete med Institutet för framstidsstudier.

WETHERALL, D. (1998) – The Growth of Archaeological Societies. *The Study of the Past in the Victorian Age*. Vanessa Brand ed. Oxbow Monograph; 73. Oxford, Oxbow Books, p. 21-34.

LE DÉBUT DE LA CULTURE DE CUCUTENI DANS L'ARCHÉOLOGIE EUROPÉENNE

Nicolae URSULESCU
Université "Al.I.Cuza", Iaşi, Faculté d'Histoire (Roumanie)

Mădălin-Cornel VĂLEANU
Complexe Muséal National "Moldova", Iasi (Roumanie)

Abstract: *In this paper are analyzed the communications on the first discoveries made at Cucuteni (1885-1889), presented by Al. Odobescu and Gr.C. Buțureanu at the Xth International Congress of Prehistoric Anthropology Archaeology (Paris, 1889) and by G. Diamandi at the Anthropological Society in Paris (1889 and 1890), as well as the role of these communications in the reception of Cucuteni culture in European archaeology.*
Keywords: 10th *Congress – Paris 1889 – Cucuteni Culture – G. Butureanu – G. Diamandi*

Résumé: *On analyse les communications sur les premières découvertes de Cucuteni (1885-1889), présentées par Al. Odobescu et Gr.C. Buțureanu au Xème Congrès International d'Anthropologie et d'Archéologie Préhistoriques (Paris, 1889) et par G. Diamandi à la Société d'Anthropologie de Paris (1889 et 1890), ainsi que le rôle de ces travaux dans la réception de la culture de Cucuteni dans l'archéologie européenne.*
Mots-clé: 10e *Congrès – Paris 1889 – Culture de Cucuteni – G. Butureanu – G. Diamandi*

Parmi les moyens de promotion des civilisations récemment découvertes, un rôle très important revient aux réunions internationales des archéologues, où il y a des possibilités de débat et de comparaison, qui aident à l'encadrement de ces civilisations dans le contexte de la Préhistoire et de la Protohistoire européenne et universelle.

Dans cette perspective, le cas de la culture de Cucuteni nous paraît exemplaire. Il s'agit d'une culture de l'Énéolithique développé, répandue sur le territoire de la Moldavie historique, entre les Carpathes Orientales et le fleuve Nistre, qui a connu une existence d'environ un millénaire (4500-3500 CAL BC). Avec les faciès apparentés de Tripolje (Ukraine) et Ariuşd (Est de la Transylvanie), la culture de Cucuteni couvre une vaste aire, approximativement 350.000 km².

Découverte en 1884[1] et explorée premièrement par deux archéologues amateurs, Nicolae Beldiceanu et Grigore Buțureanu (tous les deux professeurs dans la ville de Iaşi), la culture de Cucuteni s'est imposée assez rapidement à l'attention des spécialistes européens, d'abord par sa belle céramique peinte, mais également par la riche plastique anthropomorphe et zoomorphe en argile cuite.

Présentée quelques décennies avant la découverte d'autres cultures des Balkans comportant de la céramique peinte (en premier lieu, les cultures de Sesklo et de Dimini), la culture de Cucuteni apparaissait alors comme un phénomène historique difficilement à encadrer du point de vue culturel, chronologique et ethnique, parce qu'aucune des cultures néolithiques connues à cette époque en Europe n'utilisait la peinture pour le décor des vases; par ailleurs, les représentations plastiques en argile cuite étaient très rares et rudimentaires. Dans cette situation, les premières déterminations des découvertes de Cucuteni ont visé des périodes historiques plus récentes, d'abord le monde des Daces (Beldiceanu 1885, 1, 2, 8-9); les correspondances ont été recherchées avec quelques objets trouvés par Schliemann à Hissarlyk, Mycènes et Tirynthe (*ibidem*, 2, 4, 5). Les explications étaient recherchées surtout dans la mythologie de l'Antiquité classique (*ibidem*, 6-7).

L'importance des découvertes de Cucuteni a pu été validée par leur présentation dans la capitale spirituelle du monde de ce temps-là: Paris.

La première occasion s'est offerte lors du Xème Congrès International d'Anthropologie et d'Archéologie Préhistoriques, tenu au mois d'août 1889. Sur le conseil et avec l'aide d'Alexandre Odobescu[2] (le premier professeur d'archéologie à l'Université de Bucarest et membre du Conseil permanent du Congrès), Grigore Buțureanu (Grégoire Boutsoureano), l'un des deux professeurs de Iaşi qui avaient entrepris des fouilles à Cucuteni, a également pu participer au Congrès. Son intervention concernant les découvertes de Cucuteni a été rédigée en roumain, de sorte que la présentation au Congrès a été tenue par Odobescu en français – la langue officielle du Congrès – à la VIIème séance, le 23 août 1889 (Compte-rendu, 1891, 41). A cette occasion, Odobescu a offert un aperçu des recherches préhistoriques en Roumanie, afin

---
[1] L'anniversaire des 120 ans de la découverte de la station éponyme a été marquée par des colloques organisés à Iaşi et Piatra Neamţ. A cette occasion a été aussi lancée la monographie *Cucuteni-Cetăţuie* (des auteurs: M. Petrescu-Dîmboviţa, M.-C. Văleanu). Les travaux de ces colloques ont été publiés en deux volumes distincts (Dumitroaia *et alii* 2005; Ursulescu, Lazarovici 2006).

[2] Parmi les livres récemment parus, présentés officiellement au Congrès, on a trouvé aussi le premier volume de la monographie d'Odobescu sur le célèbre trésor de Pietroasa (Compte-rendu, p. XL).

de placer les découvertes de Cucuteni (qui se trouvaient alors dans la collection privée du professeur Beldiceanu) dans un contexte plus large (Compte-rendu, 294-298). À partir aussi des seules correspondances connues alors (celles de Schliemann au Péloponnèse et en Troyade), Odobescu considère que les découvertes de Moldavie (Cucuteni), tout comme celles de Valachie (Vădastra) et de Transylvanie (Turdaș), "semblent constituer des chaînons unissant la civilisation originaire de la Grèce et de l'Asie Mineure à celle du Caucase préhistorique" (Compte-rendu, 297). Quant aux idoles en argile cuite, on remarque spécialement l'affirmation d'Odobescu qu'en dehors d'idoles féminines, quelques-unes sont hermaphrodites (Compte-rendu, 297) – observation sera confirmée beaucoup plus tard par la mise en évidence du culte néolithique de l'androgyne (Ursulescu, Batariuc 1987; Monah 1997).

À la fin de son intervention, Odobescu exprimait sa conviction qu'un jour, l'archéologie préhistorique de Roumanie, qui présentait un réel intérêt pour la Préhistoire de l'Europe, pourrait atteindre un niveau assez élevé, et que la ville de Bucarest serait l'amphitryon d'une réunion du Congrès (Compte-rendu, 297-298);[3] son rêve s'accomplira plus tard, en 1937.

Au Congrès, Gr. Buțureanu s'est limité à présenter quelques dessins et de petites pièces originales, qu'il avait apportées à Paris (Compte-rendu, 297); mais le texte plus complet et illustré de la communication a été publié dans les actes du Congrès (Butzureano 1891, 299-307). L'auteur considère, en l'absence d'observations stratigraphiques, que toutes les découvertes de Cucuteni avaient appartenu à la même population, y compris les objets en bronze, en argent et en fer (*Ibidem*, 301). En fait, à Cucuteni, il y a des vestiges appartenant à plusieurs périodes (Schmidt 1932; Petrescu-Dîmbovița, Văleanu 2004). Néanmoins, Buțureanu a attribué correctement la plus grande partie des trouvailles effectuées sur le site (la céramique peinte, en premier lieu) à l'âge de la Pierre polie, vers le début de l'âge du Bronze (Butzureano 1891, 304). En ce qui concerne cependant l'origine de la population qui avait vécu à Cucuteni, Buțureanu croyait que celle-ci était venue d'Asie, avant de se repandre vers le Sud, comprenant tout le bassin égéen (*Ibidem*). Le mérite le plus important d'étude de Buțureanu consiste, à notre avis, dans le fait qu'il a démontré que les découvertes du type Cucuteni apparaissent aussi dans d'autres localités de Moldavie, et qu'elles formaient donc un "Kulturkreis" propre (*Ibidem*, 302, 307). C'est ainsi que la notion de ***culture de Cucuteni*** a été introduite dans l'archéologie européenne.

L'article de Buțureanu a été heureusement complété par les précisions d'Odobescu.

Les interventions d'Odobescu et de Buțureanu ont eu lieu dans le cadre du Vème thème du Congrès (*Relations entre les civilisations de Hallstadt et des autres stations danubiennes et les civilisations de Mycènes, de Tirynthe et d'Issarlik et du Caucase*), immédiatement après la communication de Schliemann, aux découvertes duquel elles se réfèrent directement (Compte-rendu, 41). Dans l'auditoire il y avait des noms célèbres de l'histoire de l'archéologie universelle: outre Heinrich Schliemann, on peut signaler la présence de Sir John Evans, de Sophus Müller, Gabriel et Adrien de Mortillet, Salomon Reinach, Hans Hildebrand, Oscar Montelius, etc. Le président du Congrès, le professeur Armand de Quatrefages, a apprécié la valeur du matériel trouvé à Cucuteni et dans les autres localités de Moldavie (Petrescu-Dîmbovița, Văleanu 2004, 17).

Une deuxième occasion favorable pour la promotion de l'importance de la culture de Cucuteni dans l'archéologie européenne est arrivée peu après, par le biais d'un jeune étudiant, George Diamandi (1867-1917). Celui-ci, après sa promotion à l'examen de baccalauréat à Iași, en 1887,[4] a effectué des fouilles personnelles à Cucuteni en 1888 (Diamandi 1889, 582). En tant qu'étudiant en droit à Paris, il a eu une intense activité de publiciste, surtout en relation avec les cercles socialistes (Ursulescu D. 1981, 483-485), mais a participé aussi, avec des communications scientifiques, aux travaux de la Société d'Anthropologie de Paris.[5] Il a publié deux de ses communications[6] dans le Bulletin de cette Société, en 1889 et 1890, informant ainsi le monde savant de l'importance des découvertes de Cucuteni. La première communication, soutenue les 7 et 21 novembre 1889, proposait, d'une manière systématique et dans un esprit interdisciplinaire, une vaste présentation de ses découvertes personnelles à Cucuteni (Diamandi 1889); dans la deuxième communication, donnée le 15 mai 1890, Diamandi livrait une série d'observations judicieuses sur quelques nouvelles idoles, trouvées dans cette station, probablement en 1889 (Diamandi 1890).

Il faut mentionner que l'apparition des deux articles de Diamady a été signalée dans la "Revue des travaux scientifiques" (t. 10, 1889, p. 860; t. 11, 1890, p. 318), qui reproduisait même leur résumé, ce qui dénote l'intérêt provoqué dans le monde scientifique par ces découvertes archéologiques.

Bien que l'auteur avait alors à peine plus de 20 ans, ses articles montrent qu'il avait assimilé de solides connaissances spécialisées (archéologie, ethnographie, anthropologie) et une pensée analytique mûre; par conséquent, ses études dépassent largement le niveau d'amateurisme qui caractérisait alors la plupart des travaux d'archéologie en Roumanie. Durant sa dernière

---

[3] Odobescu a fait la même proposition au sein du Conseil permanent du Congrès (Compte-rendu, 38).

[4] Archives Nationales – Filiale de Iași. Fonds Université – Rectorat, dossier 15/1887-1888, doc. 571-572/9-10 sept. 1887.

[5] A noter que Diamandi a donné au musée de l'École d'Anthropologie de Paris quelques objets trouvés par lui à Cucuteni (Diamandi 1889, 599).

[6] Ainsi qu'il résulte des affirmations de l'auteur (Diamandi 1889, 583), il a eu aussi d'autres interventions à la Société d'Anthropologie de Paris.

année de lycée, G. Diamandi avait d'ailleurs déjà démontré ses vastes connaissances, en publiant une étude de synthèse sur l'homme préhistorique (Diamandi 1887; Ursulescu, D. 1981, 481-482).

Dans ses études on trouve des idées qui ont le mérite de contribuer à une meilleure interprétation des découvertes de Cucuteni et à leur encadrement correct, du point de vue culturel, dans la Préhistoire et même dans le Néolithique (Diamandi 1889, 595). L'attribution culturelle se base, entre autres, sur l'étude des pièces en silex, auxquelles il reconnaît une ressemblance avec le type Robenhausen (*ibidem*, 584) – terme qui, à l'époque, désignait les découvertes néolithiques.

Compte tenu de l'état alors déficient des connaissances sur le Néolithique, Diamandi, tout comme la plupart de ses collègues archéologues, , ne pouvait pas imaginer une datation de millénaires. Datant donc la station de Cucuteni d'environ 400 av. J.-C., il fait appel, dans son analyse archéologique aux informations des auteurs antiques, qui ne pouvaient, bien sûr, expliquer les problèmes du Néolithique. Mais, d'autre part, il rejette avec fermeté les attributions ethniques fantaisistes sur l'agglomération de Cucuteni, considérée par quelques-uns comme une station grecque, dace ou slave, sur la foi de quelques correspondances apparentes. Diamandi affirme que: "En ce qui concerne la Russie, la Roumanie et l'Orient en général, je crois qu'il faut se garder un peu de ces rapprochements douteux et tâcher d'abord de trouver des jalons plus sûrs pour relier les stations les unes aux autres. Pour moi, je doute franchement, jusqu'à nouvelles découvertes du moins, de prétendues relations des colonies du Pont-Euxin avec les habitants de Coucouteni." (*ibidem*, p. 598). Il considère ainsi qu'il serait anticipé d'énoncer des hypothèses sur la population qui a vecu autrefois à Cucuteni.[7]

Diamandi combat aussi les rapprochements et les comparaisons forcées, très éloignées dans l'espace et dans le temps.[8] Ainsi, à la différence d'autres, il considère que les ressemblances entre les idoles de Cucuteni et celles trouvées par Schliemann à Troie et en Grèce ne résultent pas d'une origine commune, mais s'expliquent plutôt par les techniques de modelage imposées par la nature des objets (*ibidem*, 597-598). Afin de démontrer cette thèse, il fait appel à l'archéologie expérimentale, en modelant lui-même quelques idoles (*ibidem*, 597).

Diamandi se guidait donc selon des idées et des méthodes considérées aujourd'hui comme extrêmement modernes. Ainsi, pour éclaircir la signification de découvertes archéologiques, il fait souvent appel à des parallèles ethnographiques, qu'il trouvait surtout dans les traditions populaires des villages roumains – apparaissant ainsi comme un précurseur de l'ethnoarchéologie en Roumanie. De même, en première pour l'archéologie de Roumanie, George Diamandi met sur le tapis les données archéozoologiques et archéobotaniques de ses découvertes de Cucuteni (*ibidem*, 593).

En général, Diamandi ne se limite pas à la simple description des objets trouvés: il tente des explications et propose des classifications, comme dans le cas de la céramique, des fusaïoles et des idoles. Surtout en ce qui concerne les idoles, Diamandi revient, dans la deuxième communication, avec des explications et des parallèles pertinents: il considère que le décor de lignes incisées qui couvre le corps de quelques idoles cucuteniennes en argile cuite ne résultent pas d'un caprice de l'artiste ou de l'imitation d'un tatouage, mais qu'il représentait le vêtement particulier de la population de Cucuteni, qui aurait été très semblable à celui des Daces, des Scythes et des Gaulois (*Idem* 1890, 406-408).

Grâce à ces travaux d'une haute tenue scientifique, présentés dans des réunions scientifiques prestigieuses, les découvertes de Cucuteni ont fait leur entrée dans l'archéologie européenne. Pour preuve, des notices sur Cucuteni, ainsi que sur le faciès apparenté de Ariuşd (en Transylvanie orientale), seront très vite publiées, autour des années 1900, dans diverses études et travaux de synthèse signés par des savants réputés, comme Adrien de Mortillet (1900),[9] Eugène Pittard (1904), Hubert Schmidt (1904; 1907), Moritz Hoernes (1898; 1909), Paul Reinecke (1902), Joseph Szombathy (1894; 1895-1896), etc.

Particulièrement, l'archéologue allemand Hubert Schmidt, à la suite de ses recherches effectuées sur le matériel de Troie et des fouilles entreprises à Anau (Asie Centrale), s'est intéressé tout spécialement à la céramique peinte de Cucuteni, afin d'établir ses relations avec d'autres céramiques peintes néolithiques. Ses fouilles dans la station éponyme de Cucuteni (1909-1910), suivies de l'interprétation et de la présentation du matériel dans une ample monographie (Schmidt 1932), ont permis d'élucider de manière décisive la question de la place de la culture Cucuteni dans le Néolithique européen, et ont établi son évolution interne.

C'est ainsi que la culture de Cucuteni, grâce aux efforts conjoints des archéologues roumains et étrangers, a trouvé sa place bien méritée dans le cadre des civilisations de la Préhistoire européenne et universelle. À présent, des chercheurs de plusieurs pays (Roumanie, République de Moldavie, Ukraine, Russie, etc.) unissent leurs efforts afin

---

[7] "Il est imprudent de trop s'aventurer dans la détermination de la race qui occupa autrefois le plateau de Coucouteni. (...) Il est bon de ne pas se hâter de donner un nom aux habitants de Coucouteni." (Diamandi 1889, 598-599).

[8] "Certes, les comparaisons sont souvent profitables, mais cette méthode ne saurait toujours être appliquée sans entraîner parfois à des erreurs, et je crois que, dans certains cas, il vaut mieux chercher à expliquer les faits sur place que d'aller leur donner des solutions qui plaisent à l'esprit, mais qui s'écartent de la vérité." (Diamandi 1889, 597).

[9] Au XIIème Congrès International d'Anthropologie et d'Archéologie Préhistorique (Paris, 1900), Adrien de Mortillet a présenté la communication *Le Néolithique en Roumanie et spécialement sur la station de Cucuteni*, dans une séance présidée par Oscar Montelius (M. Petrescu-Dîmboviţa, 1940, 119).

NICOLAE BELDICEANU
(1844-1896)

GRIGORE BUȚUREANU
(1855-1907)

ALEXANDRU ODOBESCU
(1834-1895)

GEORGE DIAMANDY
(1867-1917)

d'élucider les nombreux problèmes que cette grande civilisation préhistorique soulève en permanence – comme en témoignent du reste justement les diverses interventions touchant au complexe culturel Cucuteni-Tripolje qui ont été présentées dans le cadre du XVe Congrès de l'UISPP à Lisbonne, cet automne 2006.

Références

BELDICEANU, N. (1885) – *Antichitățile de la Cucuteni. Schiță arheologică*. Iași. 9 p.

BUTZUREANO, Gr.C. (1891) – Notes sur Coucouteni et plusieurs autres stations de la Moldavie du Nord. In *Congrès International d'Anthropologie et d'Archéologie Préhistoriques. Compte-rendu de la dixième session à Paris 1889*. Paris. p. 299-307.

Compte-rendu (1891) – *Congrès International d'Anthropologie et d'Archéologie Préhistoriques. Compte-rendu de la dixième session à Paris 1889*, Paris.

DIAMANDI, [G.] (1887) – Schiță despre omul preistoric. In *Contemporanul*. Iași. V, no. 10, p. 334-345; no. 11, p. 451-459.

DIAMANDI, [G.] (1889) – Station préhistorique de Coucouteni (Roumanie). In *Bulletin de la Société anthropo-logique de Paris*. 3ᵉ série, t. 12, 4º fasc., p. 582-599.

DIAMANDI, [G.] (1890) – Nouvelles idoles de Coucouteni (Roumanie). In *Bulletin de la Société anthropologique de Paris*. 4ᵉ série, t. I, 2º fasc., p. 406-408.

DUMITROAIA, G. *et alii* (éds.). (2005) – *Cucuteni – 120 ans de recherches. Le temps du bilan*. Bibliotheca Memoriae Antiquitatis XVI. Piatra Neamţ.

HOERNES, M. (1898) – *Urgeschichte der bildenden Kunst in Europa von den Anfängen bis zum 500 v. Chr.* Wien.

HOERNES, M. (1909) – *Natur und Urgeschichte des Menschen*. Wien. 1909.

MONAH, D. (1997) – *Plastica antropomorfă a culturii Cucuteni-Tripolie*. Bibliotheca Memoriae Antiquitatis III. Piatra Neamţ.

PETRESCU-DÎMBOVIŢA, M. (1940) – Al XVII-lea Congres Internaţional de Antropologie şi Arheologie Preistorică. In *Revista de Preistorie şi Antichităţi Naţionale*. II-IV, p. 119-127.

PETRESCU-DÎMBOVIŢA, M.; VĂLEANU, M.-C. (2004) – *Cucuteni-Cetăţuie. Monografie arheologică*. Bibliotheca Memoriae Antiquitatis XIV. Piatra Neamţ.

PITTARD, E. (1904) – Ossements humains néolithiques provenant de la station de Cucuteni (Moldavie) et déposés à l'Université de Jassy. In *Bulletin de la Société des Sciences*, XII, nos. 5-6, Bucarest. p. 365-378.

REINECKE, P. (1902) – Neolithische Streitfragen. Ein Beitrag zur Methodik der Prähistorie. In *Zeitschrift für Ethnologie*. 32, p. 223-272.

SCHMIDT, H. (1904) – Troja-Mykäne-Ungarn. Archäologische Parallelen. In *Zeitschrift für Ethnologie*. 36, p. 608-656.

SCHMIDT, H. (1907) – Beiträge zur Kenntnis und zum Verständnis der jungneolithischen Gefässmalerei Sudösteuropa. In *Zeitschrift für Ethnologie*. 39, p. 121-136.

SCHMIDT, H. (1932) – *Cucuteni in der Oberen Moldau (Rumänien)*, Berlin-Leipzig.

SZOMBATHY, J. (1894) – Prähistorisches Recognoscirungstour nach der Bukowina im Jahre 1893. In *Jahrbuch des Bukowiner Landes-Museums*. II, p. 11-21.

SZOMBATHY, J. (1895-1896) – Zweite Recognoscirungstour in die Bukowina. In *Jahrbuch des Bukowiner Landes-Museums*. III, p. 20-24; IV, p. 131-135.

URSULESCU, D. (1981) – George Diamandi. In *Suceava*. VIII, p. 481-491.

URSULESCU, N.; BATARIUC, V. (1987) – L'idole androgyne de Mihoveni (dép. de Suceava). In *La civilisation de Cucuteni en contexte européen* (éds. M. Petrescu-Dîmboviţa, N. Ursulescu, D. Monah, V. Chirica). Iaşi. 1987, p. 309-312.

URSULESCU, N.; LAZAROVICI, C.-M. (coord.) – *Cucuteni 120 – Valori universale*. Iaşi.

www.ingramcontent.com/pod-product-compliance
Ingram Content Group UK Ltd.
Pitfield, Milton Keynes, MK11 3LW, UK
UKHW061214180426
11947UKWH00029B/2040